$1,000 Start-Up Workbook

Leah Ward-Lee

Published by: LWL Enterprises, Inc.
P.O. Box 16472
1997 Sadler Road
Fernandina Beach, FL 32035

All rights reserved. ISBN-13: 978-1-945484070

NOTE FROM THE AUTHOR

Starting and operating a successful business is the deal changer that puts you in control of your destiny.

- Leah Ward-Lee

Contents

SECTION I: MAKE THE DECISION

YOU'RE IN GOOD COMPANY

If you've made the decision to take this course you clearly have an interest in starting your own business. Congratulations! You're in good company. You are preparing to join those who successfully start and operate small businesses.

The Small Business Administration (SBA) in their article *Top Ten Reasons to Love US Small Business* by Robert Longley, on the www.usgovinfo.about.com website on September 4, 2015 listed those reasons as:

1. Small businesses make up more than 99.7% of all employers.
2. Small businesses create more than 50 percent of the non-farm private gross domestic product.
3. Small patenting firms produce 13 to 14 times more patents per employee than large patenting firms.
4. The 22.9 million small businesses in the United States are in virtually every neighborhood.
5. Small businesses employs about 50 percent of all private sector workers.
6. Home based businesses account for 53 percent of all small businesses.
7. Small businesses make up 97 percent of exporters and produce 29 percent of all export value.
8. Small businesses who have employees start-up at a rate of over 500,000 per year.
9. Four years after start-up, half of all small businesses with employees remain open.

10. The latest figures show that small businesses create 75 percent of the net new jobs in our economy.

FIVE REASONS TO SPEND LESS THAN $1,000 STARTING YOUR BUSINESS

Reason 1: It limits your financial exposure while you decide whether you really want to be in this particular business.

I know from personal experience how important it is to take the time to find out if you really want to be in a particular business. Before I opened a consignment store I was in a job I hated. Every spare minute I daydreamed of being a shop owner. I imagined days of happily greeting customers and helping them put together beautiful outfits.

I started out by designing my logo and branding strategy. I developed the forms I'd need to accept consignments and my inventory management system. I collected clothes my friends wanted to consign. I decided to try it out by renting a space over a weekend, printed postcards and publicized the event and did well over that weekend. So well, in fact, that the next week I quit my job and rented the space full-time.

It wasn't long before I realized the expensive space I'd rented was too small to house the inventory I'd need to even cover the rent. To try to cover just the basic expenses I kept the shop open long hours seven days a week. I hadn't considered that for every hour the shop was open I had to spend at least an hour sorting and hanging clothes and doing the consignment and business paperwork.

Finally, after going through most of my savings and ending up in a hospital because I'd spent so many hours working, I woke up and realized how much I hated being in that business.

Had I taken a part-time job in a consignment store and done better market research by talking with other consignment shop owners I could have saved myself a lot of time, energy, and money.

Reason 2: It forces you to go through the whole cycle and run the business, or as I call it, 'rinse and repeat' before you invest additional time and money.

Most businesses have busy and slow seasons. Understanding the cycle of your business insures you can deliver on your commitments to your customers without throwing money at a problem or investing too much in the wrong or unneeded material and equipment that either ends up in inventory or is wasted.

Reason 3: It allows you to learn and understand every aspect of your business since you can't afford to hire anyone, except on a limited basis, and then often only for advice.

If your business is going to grow, you'll eventually need to hire and train employees. Typically, when you hire your first employees it's so they can perform a function that frees you up to do something else. For them to know how you want that job done you'll need to take the time to show them how to do it.

Doing it yourself enough times so that you can build an employee manual and standard operating procedures goes a long way to ensuring both your business and your employees are successful and meet your expectations.

Reason 4: It teaches you to manage both your finances and your time, as you have to either keep your day job, take a part-time job, or support yourself with savings or retirement while you get your business started.

Your new business deserves the opportunity to make its way along the learning curve without the pressure of supporting anyone – even you. When both your time and you bank account are limited it forces you to invest in what's essential.

Reason 5: You might only have $1,000 to start a business … or you might not even have that much.

Exercise I-1: Why Do You Think It's a Good Idea to Only Invest $1,000 In YOUR Start-Up?

____

____

____

____

____

____

WHAT'S YOUR REASON FOR STARTING A BUSINESS?

I interviewed several hundred business owners while writing $1,000 Start-Ups. During those interviews most business owners would talk about why they started their business. Here are themes I heard repeatedly:

- I have this idea that I must try.
- My current profession doesn't pay enough.
- My current job prevents me from spending enough time with my family.
- I plan to work after retirement.
- I don't have enough saved to retire.
- I've always wanted to start my own business.
- I've always wanted to (fill in the blank) __________.
- I want to be in the driver's seat and in control of my destiny.
- I hate my job (or my boss).
- I'm unemployed.
- I'm fully employed but don't make enough to meet my financial obligations.
- I have a prison record and am having a tough time finding and keeping a job.
- I have children, parents, or a spouse who need my financial support.

Whatever your reason, to be successful as a small business owner the reason or reasons for starting a small business is personal and should be compelling enough for you to want to make the investment of time, energy, and money it will require.

Exercise I-2: The Reason(s) I Want to Start my Own Business is (are):

____

____

____

____

____

____

____

____

____

____

Mindset Tip: Try stating your reasons as something that you're moving toward rather than something you'd like to move away from. For example, "Achieving financial freedom" opens up a bright future. "Getting out of debt" while a huge relief, is about putting something behind you.

WHAT BUSINESS DO YOU WANT TO START?

Many of us start out in the workforce simply trying to make a living and look up to find ten or fifteen years have passed and we're not happy with our career choice. Often, we've tried to make a transition more than once and abandoned our dreams or put them on hold.

Years ago, Daniel Burrus, the author of The Anticipatory Organization: Turn Disruption and Change into Opportunity and Advantage (Burrus, 2017) was a guest on my radio show, *The Executive Toolbox.* As I got to know him during the pre-interview process, I realized he was one of the happiest people I'd ever met. I asked him to what he attributed his deep sense of contentment and his answer was, "I figured out the way to be happy is to find your passion and wrap a career around it."

There are those who are happy working in businesses owned by others. They want to limit the time they put into 'work' so they have time for their other passions. There's nothing wrong with that at all if that's what you want and can find work to satisfy that criteria.

Then there are those for whom the drum of their entrepreneurial spirit beats loudly. What they want is to own their own business. They might not be able to afford to quit their jobs (yet), or maybe they can, but don't want to invest a bundle until they're sure, so prefer to move cautiously down the path of business ownership. If that sounds like you, you're in good company.

Exercise I-3: A Description of the Business I Intend to Start is:

SET YOUR SMART GOAL

In Napoleon Hill's classic, Think and Grow Rich, he interviewed the most successful icons of his day and one of the conclusions he made was that to be successful you must set goals and develop a time-based plan to reach them.

Many of us start every year making New Year's resolutions. So many of us abandon them before the end of the first month it's become a cliché. As a result, many people decide not to set goals because they don't want to take the risk of not achieving them.

Be brave. Take a chance on yourself. Decide what your goals are then set yourself up for success by making them SMART goals. This phrase has been around for as long as any of us can remember, but most of us still don't structure our goals this way.

SMART goals are: Specific, Measurable, Achievable, Relevant, and Time-Based.

Specific: The goal must be specific, so you avoid false starts and time wasters. If you're like I am, when I'm well rested and take the time to examine my life I can think of ten new goals; however, I've learned that I tend to achieve only those I've taken the time to clearly define.

Instead of "I'm going to become a writer", which is indeed a goal, a specific goal would be: "I'm going to write, self-publish, and market a book and workbook that helps potential entrepreneurs start their own businesses for less than $1,000."

Measurable: It's important to state your goal so you can measure your progress toward its achievement.

I've found that the tougher a goal is and the further the finish line is from where I'm standing, the more important it is that I make the goal measurable.

So, my goal of "I'm going to write, self-publish, and market a book…." becomes "By December 31st, I will have written and self-published the $1,000 Start-Up Workbook." Now my goal starts to come to life.

Since this goal won't happen by itself, making the goal measurable forces me to develop a plan to achieve it.

Achievable: It's essential to believe your goal is achievable. If you don't believe you can accomplish it, you'll be tempted to abandon your goal when you hit the first roadblock.

I've found the best method for me to make a goal achievable is to write out the steps to achieve it and then analyze each of those steps. For example, here are the steps I wrote to get this book into your hands:

- **Step 1:** Complete first draft of the book
- **Step 2:** Edit the first draft of the book
- **Step 3:** Complete the cover, get format approval and order proof from fulfillment provider
- **Step 4:** Edit and upload changes to the proof
- **Step 5:** Publish the book and make it available for sale
- **Step 6:** Develop a business plan to market the book
- **Step 7:** Make the 1st public presentation

Once I realized I could do this in seven steps, it became achievable in my mind, particularly when I realized some of those steps involved waiting for someone else to do something. For example, Step 3. I realized while I was waiting for the proof to come in the mail, I could start working on Steps 6 and 7.

Breaking the effort down into steps helps keep any long-term goal in perspective, particularly once you realize you don't have to do anything other than take the next step toward your goal. It can be hard to see this while working full-time or looking for a job, so it's important to think of one step at a time. Take each step in its proper time and you'll reach your goal!

Relevant: The relevance of any goal is the *WHY.* If the goal isn't important enough for you to carve out time to nurture it and move it toward fruition, why choose this goal? I could go on and on about all the things we give importance to and all the things we ignore because "we have so much going on", but I trust if you look at WHY you're doing what you're doing, you'll figure it out.

When I first started as a management consultant all I wanted to do was be a successful project leader. My clients were interesting, I got to fly to their cities every week, stay in beautiful hotels, and work with fascinating people from Fortune 500 companies. I developed a solid professional reputation that ensured I was always working.

I was at the top of my game and could walk into a company and within an hour understand the three most important things that needed to change to take it to the next level. I loved the business; however, it was taking a toll on my personal life and I was increasingly troubled by the disparity of income distribution in our country.

I was frustrated at the large percent of our population who worked for minimum wage or worked full-time jobs and couldn't afford to support their families, that more than half of all people retiring had no retirement savings, and the disproportionate rate of incarceration and recidivism for the poor and for minorities.

I longed to leverage what I'd learned to help people who wanted to be successful business owners who thought owning their own business was out of reach. As a result, for years I spent my nights in hotel rooms while on consulting engagements researching and writing $1,000 Start-Ups, then writing a blog to add to that body of work. But I still kept consulting and knew I'd done nothing to make a change.

Four years after publishing the book a family crisis forced me to stop travelling for long periods of time. When I slowed down long enough to think, I knew I needed to make a change. I longed to spend time with my family, develop a sense of community, and do something to make a difference in the cause I cared so much about. I wasn't certain how to make it happen yet, but I knew it was what I wanted to do.

That's when I realized my next chapter was to develop a course that would walk potential entrepreneurs through the process of starting their own business, and devote time to making the course available to those who wanted to start their own businesses.

If your goal isn't important enough to you that you're spending every extra minute you can carve out pursuing it, ask yourself:

- Why am I pursuing this goal?
- Why is it important to me?
- Can I close my eyes and see what achieving this goal looks like?
- Am I doing this for myself or to meet someone else's expectations?

Time-Based: Once you have your specific, measurable, achievable, and relevant goal defined, you can develop a plan to get there. Assign a date to each step you defined to convince yourself your goal is achievable.

The time-based goal for writing this book became:

- **Step 1:** Complete first draft of the book – June 30th
- **Step 2:** Edit the first draft of the book – July 31st
- **Step 3:** Complete the cover, get format approval and order proof from fulfillment provider – August 31st
- **Step 4:** Edit and upload changes to the proof – September 25th
- **Step 5:** Publish the book and make it available for sale – September 30th

- **Step 6:** Develop a business plan to market the book – November 30th
- **Step 7:** Make the 1st public presentation – December 31st

Exercise I-4: State what you wrote in Exercise I-3 as a SMART goal (specific, measurable, achievable, relevant and time-based):

____

____

____

____

____

Once your smart goal is defined, write it out and place it where you'll see it at the beginning and the end of each day. Review it and recommit to it as you start each day. At the end of each day review it again and make a commitment to yourself regarding what you're going to do to help reach it the next day.

Exercise I-5: The first five steps and the dates I plan to complete them are:

Step 1: ____________________________________ **Date:** ____________

Step 2: ____________________________________ **Date:** ____________

Step 3: ____________________________________ **Date:** ____________

Step 4: ____________________________________ **Date:** ____________

Step 5: ____________________________________ **Date:** ____________

Execute Your Plan

It's important at this point to focus on Step 1. If you get caught up in how you're going to achieve every single step, you'll spend all your time figuring that out and never get started.

This happened to me while I was writing this book. I got so overwhelmed with the enormity of the effort and had so many other things going on in my life it was difficult to focus even an hour a day on getting anything done on the book. I found a million and one excuses not to just sit down and write. I realized I needed to carve out a certain amount of time each day to work on it. Once I understood that even spending an hour a day working toward my goal would help, I was able to quiet my mind enough to focus.

Excuses and distractions come easily when you first start. If you keep giving in to them, five years from now you won't be closer to starting. Sometimes you must just ask yourself whether you're willing to waste more time or if this goal is still important to you. If this happens and you recommit, rewrite your steps and reset your SMART goals.

Sometimes you'll miss the date you set for a step. When this happens, review your goal and make certain you're still committed to reaching it. If so, reset the dates and get going. If not, why not? Was it really something you wanted to do? What got in the way?

Facing these questions can and will be difficult. It's hard to face our deficiencies and mistakes. But you're strong enough and worth the effort. We owe it to ourselves and our loved ones to work to become the best versions of ourselves we can be.

SECTION II: PLAN YOUR SUCCESSFUL BUSINESS START-UP

THE IMPORTANCE AND COMPONENTS OF YOUR BUSINESS PLAN

Your business plan is a living document prepared prior to opening your business. It's used as a tool to help you focus, organize your thoughts, and make certain you've thought through every aspect of the business before you launch.

It should be updated any time there's a change in the business and at least once annually. The process of reviewing and updating your business plan on an annual basis is an exercise almost as effective as hiring a business consultant. It causes you to review the goals you set the previous year and either celebrate your successes or analyze why you didn't meet them.

It's also a communication tool you can use to show:

- A banker - if you plan to take out a loan.
- Potential investors and venture capitalists - if you want to attract outside funding.
- Building owners - if you intend to rent space.
- Suppliers – if you intend to produce custom products.
- Potential customers, particularly if you're interested in becoming a supplier to their business.

Components of a Business Plan

- **Executive Summary**: A one-page summary of everything contained in your business plan. (Since it is a summary, it's not unusual to write it last.)

- **Brief Business Description and Target Market**: This section describes the product or service you'll be offering and to whom.

- **Professional Bio(s):** Your professional bio describes your experience and achievements and how they will contribute to the success of your business. When you start your business, yours may be the only bio included in your business plan; however, as your business grows, and you add people, you'll also include bios of the management team.

- **Competitive Analysis:** This is an analysis of the top competitors in the market, a comparison of their products and services to yours, and how you will mitigate the risks to your business.

- **Marketing:** This is the business marketing plan, how you plan to let the world know about your business, and how you plan to obtain customers and clients.

- **Prototype:** This section describes the process of developing a prototype for your product or service. It also captures the cost of the prototype, in terms of time and material, providing you with the information you need to develop your financial plan.

- **Operating Plan:** This includes how you will go about setting up the business and how it will be operated.

- **Financial Plan:** This includes start-up costs, recurring costs, costs to produce the product or deliver the service, and projected sales volume.

STEP 1: BRIEF BUSINESS DESCRIPTION

Most of us intuitively know we need a business plan and have a fairly good idea of the components that need to be included but haven't yet written one because we're not sure where to start.

I've found that the best place to start is by describing the product or service you want to offer and your target market.

It's important to have a prepared response to the questions we get every day such as, "What have you been up to?" or "What kind of work do you do?" This brief description becomes the basis for your elevator speech when you're asked about the business you're starting.

You can use it to let your friends, family, and people you're meeting for the first time know you're thinking of starting your own business. You'll find it will get you valuable feedback and potential customers.

Here are some examples of brief business descriptions:

Example 1: A Virtual Florist and Gift Basket Service that operates only during the holidays. For each holiday when flowers and/or gift baskets are traditional gifts (Valentine's Day, Mother's Day, Prom/Graduation, Thanksgiving, Christmas, etc.), I plan to design and produce a limited set of arrangements and gift baskets that will be shown in a brochure. Prior to the holiday I'll show the brochure to my friends and local businesses and take orders.

Example 2: A Divorce Recovery Course, Community, & Coaching. Although there are books and support groups on Divorce Recovery, people recover at different rates, some are reticent to seek help in their community, and much of the work needs to take place individually. This online course includes a coach who also serves as facilitator and a virtual support group of people who are in the process of or have lived through a divorce.

Example 3: A Consulting Practice that works with companies whose annual revenue exceeds $10 million in the Dallas/Fort Worth, Texas and Jacksonville, Florida areas to operate more profitability by identifying and removing barriers to achieving their goals.

Example 4: A Financial Management Book and Course that teaches financial and time management to anyone who works full-time but doesn't receive a regular pay check.

Exercise II-1: Write a brief description of your business that can be used as an "elevator speech".

____

____

____

____

____

____

____

____

____

____

____

STEP 2: YOUR PROFESSIONAL BIO

Importance of Your Bio

Putting thought and energy into writing your professional bio pays big dividends. Like the resume you provide when you apply for a job, your business plan, including your professional bio, may be shared with people you haven't met. You want to be certain it provides a complete picture of who you are and represents you well.

Your professional bio should demonstrate that you have the specialized and general knowledge to launch and operate your business, provide examples of related achievements, and leave no doubt you have the personal where-with-all and strength of character to "stick with it" and be successful.

Specialized And Generalized Knowledge To Launch And Operate Your Business

Think through and make a list of the specialized and general knowledge someone starting and operating a business of this type needs to have.

If you've never worked in this type of business, go online and research businesses offering this or similar products or services.

Here are some examples of the specialized and general knowledge you'd need for several businesses.

Example 1: A Virtual Florist and Gift Basket Service

- **Specialized Knowledge:** Flower Arranging, Gift Basket Design and Assembly, Inventory Management

- **General Knowledge:** Basic Business Bookkeeping and Record Keeping

Example 2: A Divorce Recovery Course, Community, & Coaching

- **Specialized Knowledge:** Grief Coaching, Personal Change Coaching, Course Preparation, Writing, Public Speaking

- **General Knowledge:** Basic Business Bookkeeping and Record Keeping, Online Document Creation and Management Software, Online Marketing and Content Delivery

Example 3: A Consulting Practice:

- **Specialized Knowledge:** Industry or Business Experience, Project and Client Management, Change Management, Board Level Presentation Skills

- **General Knowledge:** Basic Business Bookkeeping and Record Keeping, Business Software Applications, Basic Computer Skills

Example 4: A Financial Management Book and Course

- **Specialized Knowledge:** Financial Management, Budgeting, Time Management, Personal Organizational Skills, Writing Skills, Course Preparation, Public Speaking

- **General Knowledge:** Basic Business Bookkeeping and Record Keeping, Manuscript Creation and Publishing Software, Spreadsheet Creation and Manipulation, Marketing

Exercise II-2a: List the specialized and general knowledge needed to launch and

operate your business:

____

____

____

____

____

Your Qualifications To Launch And Operate This Business

There's a reason you chose THIS business. You may have worked for a company doing this type of work or this might be the logical outcome of a long-time hobby. It might be you found a unique method or technique for solving a problem. You may have even developed a product or service that's needed in the marketplace.

Inventorying the specialized knowledge and general knowledge you have and comparing it to what you'll need will help you identify your qualifications for launching and operating this type of business. It will also help you identify whether there are qualifications you don't currently have that you might need.

List the jobs and positions you've held, events you've participated in, places you've volunteered and match what you have to the background necessary to be successful in your business.

A note at this point: If you're starting a business that requires specialized knowledge you don't have or if you have no experience in your prospective new business industry, first take the time to learn the skill or work in the industry.

Exercise II-2b: Make a list of the jobs and positions you've held, events you've participated in, places you've volunteered, and match what you did in each of these that provides you the background necessary to be successful in this business.

____

____

____

____

____

____

____

____

____

____

____

Examples of Your Achievements That Relate to Your New Business

Review each job or position you listed above. What did you improve or achieve while you were there that made the business better? Articulate results you or your team achieved that are pertinent to something you'll be doing in your new business.

This exercise reminds you of your achievements and gives you the confidence necessary to take the next step in launching your business.

Exercise II-2c: Write five short vignettes detailing your achievements and how they are pertinent to something you'll need to do in your new business.

- **Vignette 1:**

  ____

  ____

  ____

  ____

  ____

  ____

  ____

  ____

  ____

  ____

- **Vignette 2:**

- **Vignette 3:**

- **Vignette 4:**

- **Vignette 5:**

____

____

____

____

____

____

____

____

____

Why You'll Be Successful Launching and Operating This Business:

Just as important as specialized and general knowledge, pertinent experience, and achievements, is your character and ability to deliver on the commitments you make.

Examples might include service in any capacity, working while you were going to school, earning a college degree, helping to take care of siblings or parents, going to night school, helping a charity, and/or belonging to an organization.

You may also have examples of what you learned by making a mistake. Take accountability and demonstrate what you've achieved since then. You don't have to describe the mistake.

- **Example 1: Diligence:** I learned to manage my time during the four years I worked full-time attending college to earn my bachelor's degree in business.

- **Example 2: Fundraising, Marketing and Networking:** I organized an event to raise funds against domestic violence that included a "pass the purse" silent auction that collected enough to launch a 501(c)(3).

- **Example 3: Time Management:** After repeated warnings for being a few minutes late, I lost a job and learned the importance of being on-time.

Exercise II-3: Prepare three vignettes that are examples of your ability to deliver on your commitments.

- **Vignette 1:**

- **Vignette 2:**

- **Vignette 3:**

____

____

____

____

____

____

Prepare Your Professional Bio

With the information you've gathered, weave it together and write your story. The challenge is that it should be limited to one and two pages long.

Once you've finished, share it with someone you trust, get their feedback, and make edits. As with every part of your business plan you'll continue to update and personalize it depending upon the audience and where your business is in its lifecycle.

Exercise II-4: Write Your Professional Bio

____

____

____

____

____

____

____

____

____

____

____

____

____

____

____

STEP 3: CONDUCT A COMPETITIVE ANALYSIS

A competitive analysis includes identifying the top competitors in your marketspace, comparing their products, services and pricing to what you intend to offer, and planning how to mitigate those risks.

An analysis of your top competitors considers those who are currently providing the products and services in your geographical location and/or online.

Complete this analysis by doing a simple online search using Google, yellowpages.com, or yelp.com. Pick five successful businesses and compare their products and services, physical location, and marketing approaches to what you have planned for your start-up. For each criterion list your approach and theirs and, if they have the advantage, develop a mitigation strategy.

For example: they have both a bricks and mortar location and a huge online presence and you have a small email list of friends and family. Your advantage is that you don't have overhead, so you can produce your product less expensively. They have a mature product set and you have one or two products or services, therefore, you can focus on building those products using the feedback of your initial customer base.

Several years ago, I was launching a low-cost start-up and became overwhelmed by the amount of competition that already existed and had the advantage of a stable and secured customer base. The number of steps just to get my product to market felt overwhelming, and I began to doubt that I could be successful.

That changed when I realized I had the advantage of seeing what was working for them. I could leverage the work they'd done, not necessarily to compete with them, but either expand the market or develop strategies that would attract the customers I needed to get my business started.

It's important to remember you need a successful launch to start your business. Limiting your launch to a manageable set of customers or clients to ensure you can successfully deliver your product and understand the full business cycle may feel like an extra step, but it mitigates the risk of not being able to successfully deliver on a larger scale.

Four examples of competitive analyses:

- **Example 1: A Virtual Florist and Gift Basket Service that operates only during the holidays.** For each holiday when flowers and/or flower arrangements are traditional gifts (Valentine's Day, Mother's Day, Thanksgiving, Christmas, etc), I plan to design and produce a limited set of arrangements and gift baskets that will be shown in a brochure. Prior to the holiday I'll show the brochure to my friends and local businesses to get orders. I'll purchase only what I need for the orders I take and deliver the products right before the holiday.

CRITERIA	MY BUSINESS	COMPETITORS	MITIGATION STRATEGY
Bricks and Mortar Location with an Online Presence	I don't have the overhead associated with a full-service shop.	Customers can see or smell the actual arrangements.	I can offer better arrangements at a lower price.
	I must actively seek orders.	Customers either come in to shop or can order online.	My first year will be focused on building a loyal base of friends and family and face to face direct marketing with local businesses.
Established Online Florists	New Website with my own photographs.	Beautiful websites with professional photographs.	Since I must create each arrangement to photograph it, I'll build several a day two weeks prior to the holiday then deliver the arrangements to a friend or family member and photograph them receiving the arrangement. I'll limit the number of different arrangements for each holiday and post one each day before the holiday on both my Facebook Business Page and WordPress website.
	I'm an inexperienced commercial floral arranger.	They are experienced commercial floral arrangers.	I'll only create 5-6 for each holiday. I'll limit the number of holidays the first year to give me plenty of time to do the designs. Each year I'll add 5-6 new designs for each holiday to grow the standard set.
	I'm still trying to figure out how to accept online charge cards.	They have the ability to accept online charge cards.	This goes on my to-do list as something critical to learn and test prior to launch.

	I'll have a mall email list with verbal and email reminders sent prior to holidays.	They have large email lists with reminders sent prior to holidays.	I'll take my brochure with me everywhere I go prior to each holiday.
Paid Internet and Local Advertising	I have no budget for paid ads.	They routinely fund paid ads.	I'll use the flowers I purchase (wholesale) to do my designs as marketing tools and gifts to remind people of my business, and for photo opportunities.

- **Example 2: A Divorce Recovery Course, Community, & Coaching:** Although there are books and support groups on Divorce Recovery, everyone recovers at a different rate, people are often reticent to seek help in their community, and much of the work needs to take place individually. This online course provides a virtual support group of people who are in the process of, or have just lived through, a divorce with a coach for support.

CRITERIA	MY BUSINESS	COMPETITORS	MITIGATION STRATEGY
Bricks and Mortar Location	My business will not be religiously based, therefore, I must build a community instead of leveraging the church community.	They are most often religiously based with a built-in community.	I'll launch to a small circle of friends who have reviewed the material. I'll tell them about the product, ask for their help by telling their friends who might need this type of support about it.
Online Courses	My course is an online course, cohort, and moderated sessions.	They are online courses and communities; however, no cohort or moderated sessions.	I'll develop the course and write a weekly blog to build a community and offer 12-week moderated sessions.

- **Example 3: A Consulting Practice** that works with companies whose annual revenue exceeds $10 million operate more profitabaly by working with them to identify and remove barriers blocking their goals.

CRITERIA	MY BUSINESS	COMPETITORS	MITIGATION STRATEGY
Marketing	Although I have more than 20 years experience, I've sub-contracted to firms who have a sales presence and am not starting out with a website.	They cite experience with previous engagements and results on their websites.	I'll write a blog containing vignettes of issues clients faced and the tools used to improve their probability of success. I'll also include what I've done and the results my clients attained on my Linkedin profile page. Additionally, I'll develop a course that teaches consultants and companies how to use the tools to achieve results.
Price	I plan to target companies with at least $10m in annual revenue for Analyses and target employees of those firms by offering courses that teach the tools.	During the Analysis phase firms offer lower rates. I found rates from $7k-$14k per man week.	For the first five Analyses I'll charge $2.5k per man week for at least 2 people per week and complete a single location, single product line business in 3 weeks.
Sales	For 20 years I've received referrals from other consultants.	They typically have dedicated sales forces	I'll complete and release workbooks of the tools and use Linkedin to target local companies for 3-week assessments that help them develop an executable plan. Additionally I plan to develop a series of seminars and promote them locally.
Geographical Reach	I'll limit engagements to my geographical areas.	Most firms target clients in the US and worldwide.	This allows me to gain visibility as a local speaker, from local referrals, and through the Chamber of Commerce.
Online Courses	I plan to offer online courses, a cohort, and moderated sessions.	They offer online courses; however they typically offer no cohort or moderated sessions.	I plan to develop the course and write a weekly blog to build a community. Offer 4-week moderated sessions to solve specific issues.

- **Example 4: A Financial Management Book and Course** that teaches financial and time management to anyone who works full-time but doesn't receive a regular pay check.

CRITERIA	MY BUSINESS	COMPETITORS	MITIGATION STRATEGY
Product	I plan to write and self-publish a book and workbook that teaches financial and time management to anyone who works full-time but doesn't receive a regular paycheck.	The space is extremely crowded with advice for people who earn a regular income but not for people who don't. Dave Ramsey and Suzy Orman are two of the biggest.	I plan to leverage 20 years of experience and Facebook following of more than 1,000 in the bar and food services industry.
Marketing	I plan to use social media, podcasts, and word of mouth, particularly in my geographical area.	They use radio shows, TV appearances, infomercials, and podcasts.	I plan to create a small targeted email list, build a series of product launch messages and videos, obtain local bars as sponsors, offer 10-week courses, as well as an ongoing weekly podcast.
Website	I'm building my own website.	They have mature websites with large following and sponsors.	Facebook business website (by invitation only) and WordPress websites with weekly blog, sponsors, and affiliates
Online Courses	I plan to offer both online and local courses, a cohort, and moderated sessions.	They offer only online and self-study courses.	Develop courses and write a weekly blog to build a community. I also plan to offer 10-week moderated sessions.

Exercise II-5: Conduct a Competitive Analysis for YOUR Business and Record the Results in the Table Below:

CRITERIA	MY BUSINESS	COMPETITORS	MITIGATION STRATEGY

STEP 4: DEVELOP YOUR MARKETING PLAN

Your marketing plan doesn't have to be lengthy or verbose. Use a structured approach and commit it to paper to help focus your marketing efforts and determine where to spend your marketing dollars. It also provides you with something tangible you can share with advisors who may have ideas that will help accelerate your business growth.

If you have a computer, you can design most of the marketing materials yourself, at least when you're starting your business. I recommend you prepare your own marketing materials the first time, even if you simply draw them or write them out on plain paper. This reduces the cost enormously, particularly since the information typically matures over time as you develop the look and feel of your brand.

Target Market

You began the process of defining your target market when you completed your competitive analysis.

A clear definition of your target market helps focus your marketing efforts. At the highest level there are two terms that help you get started with refining that definition:

- **B to B (Business to Business):** This type of business sells products or services to other businesses.

- **B to C (Business to Consumer):** This type of business sells products or services to consumers.

Typically, you market your product differently when you're selling directly to the consumer of a product versus when you're selling to other businesses who are using your product or service or selling to the consumer. Your target market could be both – you may market in different places or use a different approach for each.

The next step is to define specifically who will use the products or services your company offers. Jeff Walker, whose book Launch, an Internet Millionaire's Secret Formula to Sell Almost Anything Online, Build a Business You Love, and Live the Life of Your Dreams, uses the term "avatar" to describe his typical prospect.

Your imaginary customer, or avatar, is the person you imagine when you're developing your marketing approach. Defining your target market is essential if your marketing approach is to focus on their needs, where they find new products, and how they're influenced to buy. I've found it helps to use the method reporters use to ensure a newspaper story covers all the bases by answering: "Who, What, Where, When, Why, and How" to zero in on the market you're trying to reach.

- **Who:** Developing a mental picture of a member of your target market can help give your marketing plan focus. Although there are always outliers, a person's profession, age, gender, geographical location, and economic status are predictors when determining their interest in your product and where they will go to find information about your product. Does your avatar have a certain profession or hobby, work full-time for a company, or own his/her own business? Is he/she a parent or grandparent? Who influences his/her buying decision?

- **What:** What would this person gain by using your product or service? What would he/she be looking for in a product or service like yours? What would influence the decision to buy? What triggers the purchase? What will be better for him/her with this product or worse without it?

- **When:** When would he/she shop for your product? Would it be during or after business hours, on weekends, or on holiday? Will the person buy it when he/she hears about it or sees it or seeks out it out on his/her own?

- **Where:** Where would your avatar learn about it? Where would he/she buy it? Where and how does he/she hear about products or services like yours? Where would he/she use this product?

- **Why:** Why would he/she buy your product or service? Why would he/she buy it from you? Why does he/she need your product? Is his/her need for this product based on an event that's occurring in his/her life (engagement, new baby, home remodeling, retirement, holiday), a situation they want to change (starting a business, improving financial situation, getting fit, eating better), or something he/she use all the time (shampoo, cleaning service, lawn service)?

- **How:** How much could your avatar afford to spend for your product or service? How will your avatar use it?

Exercise II-6: Describe Your Target Market

- **Who:**

  ____

  ____

  ____

  ____

- **What:**

  ____

  ____

  ____

  ____

- **Where:**

  ____

  ____

  ____

  ____

- **When:**

  ____

  ____

  ____

  ____

- **Why:**

  ____

  ____

  ____

  ____

- **How:**

  ____

  ____

  ____

  ____

Basic Marketing Tools

There are a set of low-cost basic marketing tools available to every business owner.

- **Business Name:** Your business name should describe your business. Keep it short and memorable.

- **Elevator Speech:** This is what you tell someone when they ask about your business. A good elevator speech describes your business and the benefits you provide your customers in less than twenty seconds.

- **Logo:** You can have your business logo designed by a graphics designer, pick one from one of the many Internet sites that offer standard logos you can customize, such as www.avery.com, or design one yourself. If you go to the website and search business cards, there are almost 400 designs to choose from. You can also go to any of the office supply stores who offer business card printing services and they will have additional logos to choose from.

- **Standards/Branding:** Every form you use and email you send is an opportunity to market your business. Pick a font and a style and use it on everything you print. It helps 'brand' your business.

- **Business Card:** This is what you leave with someone after you tell them about your business. It should have the name of your company, your name, your telephone number, and your email address. If you have a website, it should include the URL. When you first start out, you can buy business cards in a multitude of inexpensive ways. You can go to an office supply store and buy the card stock and design and print them yourself or you can have someone at the store design and print the cards for you. Additionally, there are online services that allow you to design your card, print, and send them to you.

- **Brochure:** A simple trifold brochure that lists the services you provide or shows examples of your products and includes your contact information is used by many business owners as a sales tool. Most office supply stores will help you design and print the brochure. Additionally, the manufacturers of the paper stock provide templates you can use to design and print your own.

- **Your 'Book':** Your 'book' is a collection of examples of your products or services. If you are selling a product, you will need to have a set of examples you can photograph (and put in your brochure, book, or website) to show to potential customers. If you are marketing a service, you'll want to describe the service.

- **Examples/Testimonials:** The tough part about starting out is that you haven't sold your products or services yet, but you know what problem this product or service will solve or what need it will fulfill. Make sure this is a short-term challenge by collecting examples or testimonials as you go.

- **Magnetic Signs:** These are the signs that go on the driver's and passenger's door of your vehicle to advertise the name of your company and display your contact information. They are surprisingly inexpensive.

- **Follow-Up:** It's common knowledge in marketing that it costs five times as much to get a new customer as it does to get repeat business from an existing customer, so ensure you have a plan for how you're going to stay in touch with your client base. It could be something as simple as an annual holiday card, but plan how you're going to do this before you open for business.

- **Repeat Business:** It's also said that the most important sale to a customer is the second because it lets you know a customer was happy enough with your service or product to come back. Your strategy here can run the gamut from asking them if they were satisfied in person or a follow-up email asking them to rate your product or service. Even more effective is a coupon with a percent savings they can use on their next purchase and an additional discount for a referral.

- **Press Release:** When you open your business or offer a new product or service, you should write a press release and send it to your local media.

There are hundreds of online services that will distribute your press releases, some are free and some charge.

Exercise II-7: Describe the Basic Marketing Tools You'll Use in Your Business

____

____

____

____

____

____

Basic Venues For Marketing:

- **Friends and Family:** Of course, you'll tell your friends and family about your business. They're the people who will help promote your business to their friends and extended family. Treating them like the assets they are, particularly when they offer feedback, is a skill to cultivate.

- **Professional Colleagues:** If you're starting a business whose products or services would interest previous colleagues, let them know. A phone call, personal email, or holiday card containing a handwritten note can get you the business you need to get started.

- **Door to Door:** Flyers, postcards, or advertisements in local circulars can result in new customers or clients. Keep track of the cost and time it takes to do each 'campaign' and be sure the cost justifies the number of inquiries you get as a result. Conducting a one-time event or providing a limited time offer, such as a coupon, can increase the number of responses.

- **Homeowner's Associations:** The description of some products or services are appropriate for inclusion in a newsletter or as an article your neighbors would be interested in reading.

- **Suppliers:** Your suppliers are a great source of referrals. Be certain to treat them like potential customers. Ask them who they know who would be interested in your service or product.

- **Affiliated Businesses:** These are businesses who share the same target market. For example: a landscaping business and realtor both target homeowners, and pet hotel manufacturers and pet shop owners target people who have dogs or cats. Make a list of every type of business that shares the same target market, then develop methods for getting and staying in touch with those business owners.

- **Chambers of Commerce:** Most Chambers have a weekly or monthly morning breakfast for small business owners to get together and network. Usually there's a nominal fee, but typically you don't have to even join to be able to attend. Usually each business owner gets a minute or two to stand up, give their elevator speech, and there's time at the end to talk with each other and collect leads.

- **Public Venues:** You may be able to talk about or sell your products and services at public venues such as libraries, recreation centers, or schools. If they're already planning an event, find out what it costs to be included. If not, offer to organize an event.

- **Commercial Venues:** Office buildings, malls, or lobbies of any kind already have people passing through who may be interested in your product or service.

- **Farmers Markets:** Weekly markets aren't just for produce anymore. Consider these if you have a product to sell that can be displayed in a small area.

- **Arts and Crafts Fairs:** Contact the fair organizer to find out the cost to display. Determine how many of your products you would have to sell to cover the cost of the display fee. If it's reasonable, try it.

Exercise II-8: Describe the Basic Marketing Venues You'll Use for Your Business

___

___

___

___

___

___

Your Virtual Presence:

- **Website:** Depending on the type of business you open you may decide to build a website. Having a website is an inexpensive way of legitimizing your business. There's becoming an expectation for every business to have one.

- **Domain Name:** The first step is to select your domain name. Even if you're not going to build a website immediately go ahead and do this – particularly if you're going to have a business email address. Type the name you've selected into your browser and see what you get.

  If a website comes up, you know that domain name is not available. Find something else.

  If you get a message such as, 'the name is available, register here', there's a good possibility the name is available.

  If you're going to include building a website as part of your business launch, wait until you select the company you're going to use to host your website before registering the name. Hosting companies often offer lower costs for registering your domain name through them.

- **Types of Websites:** The simplest type of website has static information, that is, information that doesn't change. It's basically just a different layout of a brochure that shows examples of your work, testimonials from satisfied clients, and your contact information.

  More complicated websites contain not only static content but also links to related content, the ability to order and pay for products, and buttons that, when selected, redirect the surfer to another page or website that is affiliated in some way.

  Look at your competition's websites. Note the features and type of website they are using and select what will most effectively market your business.

- **Hosting Sites that Offer Design Tools:** The next step is to choose the company who's going to host your site and the tool you're going to use to build it. It doesn't need to be an expensive or complicated proposition, but it's essential that you do your research carefully.

  Companies such as BlueHost, WordPress, Weebly, and Justhost, provide tools that allow you to build your own website without coding or technical skills.

  Type 'how do I build a website' into your browser and these and other companies will be listed. Research them by going to their sites and reviewing the capabilities.

  For each of the hosting services you're considering type 'complaints' and the name of the service provider to evaluate what other people say about their experience. Also look to see if the company has a user's group or an online forum.

- **Establish Your Internet Presence:**

  The last step before you register your domain name is to verify that you will receive 3 – 5 email addresses as part of the package. Then:

  - Select the hosting service and register your domain name.
  - Set up your email addresses using either your name or position and the format: yourname@yourcompanyname.com.
  - Build your website.

- **Search Engine Optimization:** There are dozens of search engines available today, with Google leading the way. You want to be sure potential customers can find your business when they're looking for the products or services you offer.

  - **Keywords:** The most straight forward method is to be certain you use keywords that are the same words someone would use when looking for your product or service.

- ➢ **Update Content Frequently:** Search engines are notified when content is updated and will search your website again to 'discover' what's there. This activity moves your website up in the order of websites that have the keyword a person searching used.
- ➢ **Google's Free Search Tool:** Google has a search tool that provides ratings on the competition, how many global monthly searches occurred, and the number of searches by keyword and phrases. It takes some time to learn to use this tool; however, if your business success is largely dependent on Internet traffic, it's worth it.

- **Register Your Internet Presence:** We've all noticed how seldom we use the Yellow Pages anymore. They have been replaced with online directories. You can go to any of the major search engines and type: 'how to list a business' to get instructions.

- **Social Media:** Social media has lost some of its luster; however, it's still a tool to use to market your business. As a small business owner your time is your most valuable commodity, so ensure you find a reasonable balance.

  - ➢ **Linkedin:** As of this writing, Linkedin is the most accepted social media venue for professionals. If customers will be drawn to your business because of your professional background, it may be worthwhile to spend some time keeping your profile current. You should also:

    - o Update your profile with information about your new business. You can set a trigger that sends out a profile update to everyone in your network.
    - o Endorse other people.
    - o Look for people who are connected to your connections and who are in your target market. Send your connections notes asking for introductions.

- **Facebook:** Facebook has a business arm at www.facebook.com/business that lets you send ads and notices to your clients and customers. If you decide to use your personal Facebook page, make sure it represents who you want to be and how you want to represent your business.

- **YouTube** (www.YouTube.com): If you have a product or service that would benefit from video marketing, this is the site for you.

- **Twitter** (www.twitter.com): You can use Twitter to send 140-character tweets to announce events, sales, or other marketing messages.

- **Pinterest** (www.pinterest.com): You can share pictures of your products on Pinterest with a link to your website. Other viewers can 'Pin' your images.

- **Squidoo** (www.squidoo.com): Largely focused on content sharing, it has articles on just about everything. You can contribute articles that contain links to products you're selling or back to your website.

Exercise II-9: Describe the Virtual Marketing Presence You'll Establish and Operate for Your Business

____

____

____

____

____

____

STEP 5: BUILD YOUR PROTOTYPE

Purpose of a Prototype

Your prototype is a model of the product or service you're going to be selling. Building a prototype is a critical step in the life of your business because:

- It takes you from conceptual to actual
- It sets a baseline for your production costs
- It provides you with the information needed to understand your constraints in terms of time, money and capacity.

Let's explore each of these in detail.

From Conceptual to Actual

Whether your business produces a product, like our example of Holiday Florists, or service, like the Consulting Practice, you'll have one-time activities while you're starting up and activities to complete each time you produce a product or deliver a service.

Set a goal so that you'll spend no more than $100 of your start-up money building your prototype. This will help you avoid the tendency of most business start-ups to invest in tooling, items, or supplies they don't need. It's amazing how creative and resourceful you can be when you limit the amount of money you intend to spend.

- **Design.** For both products and services write a description of the purpose, benefits, and criteria for success.

  - **Product:** If it's a product, sketch out your idea or use any one of the software products you have for a drawing. On the design or spreadsheet list each component you'll need, how many, and a brief description of the component.
  - **Service:** If it's a service or set of services, design the process you'll use to deliver each one.

- **Space.** You will need enough space to build and store your work-in-process (WIP). Your starting space should have no cost or an extremely low cost.

  Identify and clear the space you're going to use to build your product or design your service offering. Many new business owners start by using their dining room table and store their whole business in a box. Some are lucky enough to be able to designate a specific space in an office, garage, or basement where they can work.

  - **Product:** Designate space to store your inventory. If you need space you don't have, such as space that's refrigerated or a commercial kitchen, determine how you can obtain this to build your prototype.

    If you're going to need pictures of your finished product, identify where space is available and determine what type of backdrops you'll need. An inexpensive piece of material or a tablecloth from a second-hand store thumbtacked to the wall with a cardboard box underneath it is often all you'll need to create a professional effect.

    These photographs will be used for your brochure or website and will be what your customers see when they're shopping and deciding whether to buy your products or services. Store them electronically with the product name (if you have multiple products) and the date.

  - **Service:** Regardless of whether you're going to perform the service(s) you'll be offering remotely (from a home office), at a customer's site or in a rented space, establish where you'll build your prototype, so you can keep everything you'll need together.

- **Tools, Fixtures, and Equipment.** Use what you have first, those that are free, then those you can borrow from friends or family, then look in thrift stores or on sites such as Craigslist or eBay. If there are businesses in your town using the tools, fixtures, and equipment you need, see if you can rent them when their businesses are closed.

- **Consumable/Non-Consumable Items.** Identify wholesale suppliers for each item you need. Comparison shop for perishable and non-perishable items online and by visiting local wholesalers, if possible. Once you identify a supplier for each component, add the supplier's name, stock keeping unit (SKU) number, price, and quantities at which you get each price break to the information collected when you were doing your design. If you identify more than one supplier who provides a product, add a line for them as well. This is the start of your supplier's list and bill of materials (for consumable items) and inventory (for non-consumable items).

If you haven't yet registered your business and received a Tax ID number (check state requirements), you probably won't be able to purchase items for the wholesale price and you'll have to pay tax on what you purchase to build your prototype.

Once you've identified where you're going to purchase items for your prototype, make the purchases. Total the cost for what you purchased to complete one item and enter it into your bill of materials.

If you had to purchase more than one of any item or purchased anything you didn't use, you have the start of an inventory of components you can use for subsequent products.

In other words, your bill of materials shows what you need to build a product and your inventory lists what you have on-hand and items you have that are non-consumable.

- **Build or Assemble Your Prototype.** As you're doing this, take the time to write each step down and how you completed it. Although these steps may change over time, when your business starts to grow you will need to train employees on how to do what you do.

    - **Product:** Record the steps required and the time it takes for each as you complete them using a stopwatch (there's one on most phones). When you've finished, record the total time for production. These become the baseline for your time standards and the start of your **work instructions.**

    - **Service:** Your work instructions are important if your business provides a service. As you walk through your prototype you'll be able to identify not only the steps in the process but how each step should be completed.

- **Test Your Prototype.** Test your product or service against your written definition of the design, purpose, and criteria for success.

    Friends, family, and professional colleagues are a great resource for this and can make valuable suggestions to help you improve. Often, however, you must "give them permission" to give you honest feedback.

    After asking them if the product or service met the design, purpose, and criteria for success, ask them how much they'd be willing to pay for this product or service.

- **Set Your Price.** During your competitive analysis you determined what your competitors were charging for their products. Your price should be competitive and cover the cost of producing the product and/or delivering the service.

    The price should also be high enough to cover your overhead and profit, which is often difficult to determine at this point. A rule of thumb is that the sum of your material and labor cost should be only half of the selling price once you're open for business.

Example of a Product: Holiday Florists Mother's Day Bouquets

- **Design Six Mother's Day Bouquets.** Each bouquet should delight the recipient, include care instructions, be worth the sales price, and last for a minimum of five days.

  Develop a catchy name for each bouquet. Under each name on the design, list the perishable and non-perishable items for each. After you've done a preliminary design for each bouquet, research the wholesale price of each component.

BOUQUET NAME: ____

SALES PRICE: ____________ **TOTAL COST:** __________

ITEM DESC	QTY	SUPPLIER	STOCK KEEPING UNIT (SKU)	UNIT COST	TOTAL COST

- **Set-Up Space for Assembly and to Store Work in Process.** Clear a table or workbench for assembly and make space in your refrigerator to store your flowers.

- **Identify Minimum Tooling and Fixtures.** Because flowers are perishable, you'll need a method to keep them at the proper temperature from the time they're purchased, transported to your workspace, consumed as components of bouquets, and delivered to the customer. You'll also need a stand to hold the bouquet while you're arranging the flowers and photographing the completed arrangement. Your tools at this point will be minimal. You'll need pliers, clippers, and gloves.

- **Standard Non-Perishable Items for Six Bouquets.** Total the list of items from each of the bouquets using the lists developed during the design phase. Make a list of the standard items you'll need, such as florist's tape, wrapping paper, and ribbon. Then add the specific colors and descriptions of what you'll need for the specific holiday, in this case Mother's Day.

- **Perishable Flower Stock for Six Bouquets.** Make a list of the number and type of flowers you'll need for the each bouquet.

- **Minimum Photography and Printing Capability for Six Mother's Day Bouquets.** Make a list of what you'll need to photograph each bouquet, including the camera (or cell phone), printer, ink and paper for creating your brochure.

- **Choose Your Test Group.** Determine who your test group will be. Contact them to be certain they'll be available on the day you'll have your bouquets ready.

- **Shop for the Prototype.** With a limit of $100, shop for everything you'll need for your prototype, purchasing the perishable items last. When you get back to your workspace, put everything where you'll need it to use it.

- **Assemble and Photograph the Prototypes:** Use a stopwatch and record how long it takes to complete each step.

- **Assemble Your Test Group.** Get their feedback and suggestions on each bouquet and the price of each. Photograph a member of your test group receiving each bouquet and let them keep it.

- **Adjust Your Production Designs (if needed).** Based on the feedback you receive, adjust your designs with the understanding that you'll have to build another prototype to photograph.

Example of a Service: Consulting Practice

- **Define the Service.**

The firm will offer organizational assessments to companies who want or need to increase their profitability. At the end of the assessment the client will have:

- A clearly defined **goal** and goal alignment at the executive level.
- A clear understanding of the **current state** and the opportunities there are to reach the goal.
- A complete description of the **future state** as it pertains to the people, processes, and tools.
- A detailed, executable **plan** of how to get there.
- Quantifiable and measurable statement of the **cost/benefit** of the plan.

Develop and organize the collateral and studies you would use to offer an organizational assessment: Goal Development, Current State Alignment, and Future State Vision.

- **Space** Product and collateral development, scheduling, and back office administration will be done from the home office. Client delivery will be conducted at the client site.

- **Minimum Equipment** The Microsoft Office Suite will be used to produce all collateral. Personal laptop computers will be used by all consultants both in the home office and on client sites. All laptops much be equipped with virus and security software. The HP7600 will be used to produce 11"x17" client 'maps' for delivery.

- **Consumable/Non-Consumable Supplies** Printer paper and ink.

- **Develop the Practice Collateral.** For each practice area:
  - Create a Practice Folder on the share drive.
  - Develop a set of vignettes from previous engagements that describe the situation, detail the intervention, and report the results.
  - Develop written instructions on how to use each tool associated with that engagement and store the tool and instructions in the "Tools" folder.

- Develop a Power Point depiction of the steps associated with each vignette's workstream and a key event schedule.

- **Identify the Test Group, Solicit Feedback, and Incorporate the Feedback into the Collateral.** Identify and contact trusted professional colleagues who can provide feedback for the collateral.

Production Cost Baseline

Your baseline production cost is the cost of producing one unit of each of your products or services stated in dollars and time.

For a product-based company like Holiday Florists, this is the cost of goods sold, and incremental time required to make and deliver each bouquet. However, it doesn't include the overhead cost of the tooling or overhead time associated with designing the bouquets, finding the suppliers, and shopping for and transporting the materials.

For a service company like the Consulting Practice, this cost includes the daily rate paid to consultants delivering the analysis, the cost of printing client specific materials, and the cost associated with transportation to and from the client site. The time to develop the collateral and the costs associated with sales is considered overhead.

Exercise II-10: Plan and Build Your Prototype

- **Production Cost Per Unit** ____________
- **Production Time Per Unit** ___________

STEP 6: DEVELOP YOUR FINANCIAL PLAN

Your start-up costs are what you'll need to spend to open your business, produce, and market your first set of products or services.

Basic Start-Up Expenses

There are some basic start-up expenses needed to open most businesses.

- **Business Registration and Licensing (≈$100):** Most small businesses need a combination of licenses and permits from federal, state, and in some cases, county agencies. The requirements and fees vary based on your business activities, location, and government rules.

- **Computer, Printer, & Software (≈$400):** If you already have access to a computer and printer, great. If you don't, refurbished computers, monitors, and printers can be purchased from Amazon.com or larger chains of office supply stores at a very low cost.
  You'll also need basic software such as Microsoft Office and a set of virus software.

- **Basic Marketing Materials (≈$100):** By printing your basic marketing materials such as business cards and brochures yourself, the cost will be limited to ink and paper.

- **Prototype and Start-Up Inventory for Businesses that Sell Products (≈$300):** If you're selling a product you'll need to build a prototype and a limited set of initial products to sell.

- **Website and Web Hosting for Businesses that Market Services (≈$100):** If you're opening a business selling a service, plan to spend this amount to launch your website.

  If your business sells a product or set of products, it's important that there is enough profit from each product you sell to cover the cost of producing the product and some portion of your operating costs.

- **Banking (≈$40):** You can open a basic business account with as little as $25 and many of the major banks will charge $15 a month in service fees. With this type of account, you'll typically be provided an ATM card.

Exercise II-11: Estimate Your One-Time Start-Up Costs

CATEGORY	AMOUNT

Operating Costs

Operating costs are the recurring costs of operating your business. As a low-cost business start-up, it's essential to minimize your operating costs until the business is up and running and you're making sales.

Typical operating costs, including those associated with operating a storefront or office space, should be avoided until you have enough business to not only pay yourself, but support yourself with the profit from this business.

There are some operating costs, however, that are prudent for many types of businesses:

- **Insurance/Bonding:** For services businesses that include operating on someone's residential or business property such as handyman, window washer, or housekeeper, plan on paying monthly insurance premiums and being bonded.

  If you're using your vehicle in your business, it's important to notify your insurance company and provide an estimate of how many miles you'll be driving for business.

- **Bank Fees:** You should plan to spend at least $15 per month in service fees.

- **Website Hosting Fees:** If your business provides a service or is virtual and you have a website you'll incur monthly hosting fees.

Exercise II-12: Estimate Your Monthly Recurring Overhead Costs. Total monthly recurring overhead costs and then compare it to the amount of start-up funding you still have available to provide you the information you need to understand how long you have until you need to complete enough order to cash cycles to earn enough to pay your overhead costs and to buy what's needed to fund the purchase of the next cycles of materials or additional services. It's tough to estimate your revenue the first year; however, what's important is estimate the value and number of sales required to cover your overhead expenses.

CATEGORY	AMOUNT
TOTAL MONTHLY OVERHEAD	

STEP 7: DEVELOP YOUR OPERATING PLAN

Developing an operating plan can seem daunting when all you have is a concept of how your business will operate; however, this process enables you to think through your plan and build a roadmap from concept to reality.

Understanding Your Operating Constraints

- **Money** is often the most pressing constraint for start-ups.

    - **Product:** Not surprisingly, a prototype is typically the most expensive unit you produce because it's the first. Knowing the cost will determine how many units of your product you can afford to produce for your initial product offering.
    - **Service:** Most of the cost of any licenses, products, or tools you require are typically one-time costs or paid annually and not an incremental cost for each customer. (These will be discussed during Step 7.)

- **Time** is typically the second most pressing constraint. When you build your prototype, you are also documenting the process and determining how long it will take to build each unit or deliver service to a customer.

When you're starting up you're doing everything for the first time. Working through the learning curve of "firsts" will take longer for the first ten units than it will for the next.

- **Space** is typically the third constraint. Understanding how much product you have space for or how many customers you can accommodate is essential to developing your operating plan.

The key to managing your constraints is ensuring your order to cash cycle is well defined and as short as possible.

Define Your "Order To Cash" Cycle

Simply put, your order to cash cycle is the chronological set of steps in the process from taking an order to delivering the product or service and receiving payment.

Mapping out and describing the steps provides the opportunity to understand what's required for each step. In the following example for Holiday Florists I've highlighted the collateral material and forms needed for each step.

Example 1-Product: Holiday Florists Mother's Day Campaign

- **Obtain Orders and Collect Payments**

Two weeks before Mother's Day, the business owner plans to take the simple **brochure** that shows the bouquet options for Mother's Day to friends and family first and then to local businesses she frequents. She will obtain orders using an **order form** that includes the ordering individual's name, telephone number, address, email address, and payment information. The order form also includes the recipient's name, telephone number, delivery address, and email address.

When ordering the customer can pay with cash, check, credit card, or electronic payment.

As part of the ordering process the customer fills out a **card** that will go with the order to personalize the gift.

- **Purchase Non-Perishable and Perishable Stock**

The week before Mother's Day, the business owner completes the **shopping list** based upon the set of orders received. She purchases the non-perishable items first and the perishable items second.

- **Transport to Assembly Area**

Non-perishable items are purchased during the first shopping trip and transported to the business area. Because the flower market opens early in the morning, flowers are purchased at the beginning of the day, placed on ice in the delivery vehicle, and transported back to the refrigerated section of the assembly area.

- **Confirm Deliveries and Assemble Bouquets**

The recipients on the **delivery list** of orders to be delivered Thursday are called on Wednesday to confirm their availability Thursday afternoon during the delivery window of time. During these calls any requests for delivery on Friday or Saturday are moved to those days. Friday deliveries are then confirmed on Thursday, and on Friday the remaining orders are confirmed. Any unconfirmed orders require further contact with the person who ordered the flowers.

Thursday before Mother's Day is the first assembly day and one third of the orders are assembled each day through Saturday. As bouquets are completed they are placed in the refrigerated staging area for delivery late afternoon.

- **Confirm and Deliver Orders**

The delivery process includes getting permission from and taking a picture of the person who received the flowers, then **emailing** the picture to them and the person who ordered the flowers on Mother's Day.

Example 2-Service: Consulting Firm

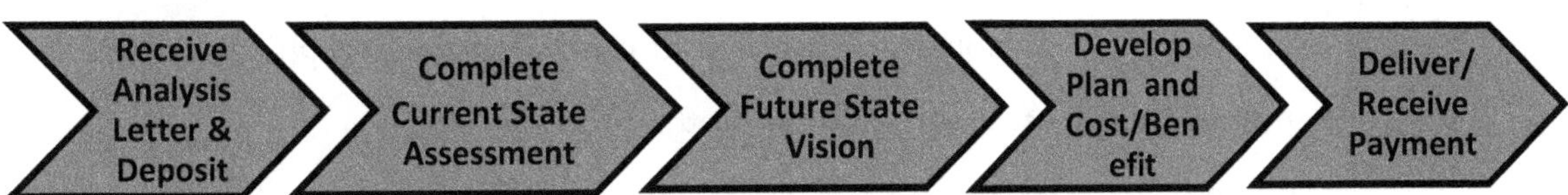

- **Receive Analysis Letter, Confirm and Deliver Orders**

Receipt of a signed letter and deposit for 25% of the cost of the Analysis is the start of the Order to Cash process. (The collateral and processes used to get the sale, retain the client, and train and pay consultants are back office functions that will be discussed in Section III.)

The Consulting Firm then provides the client with a Prep List and Data Request for the Analysis.

During this step, the starting and ending dates of the Analysis and all meetings are scheduled with the client, the executive team is provided samples of organizational communications, and the purpose and goal of the Analysis is communicated or relayed throughout the organization.

- **Complete Current State Assessment**

The Current State Assessment includes studies that will help the organization understand their current state and opportunities that should be addressed to achieve their goal. Studies include:

- A survey used to determine whether the organization is ready, willing, and able to change.
- Executive Interviews with all key executives and stakeholders of the organization.
- An assessment of the efficacy of how the organization is managed through the Plan, Do, Check, Act cycle.
- An assessment of how information and product flow through each functional and production area, and throughout the organization.
- Based on what is learned from studies completed the first four days, a study that demonstrates and quantifies the magnitude of the most significant opportunity is conducted.

The studies are packaged and presented to the executive team at an Executive Meeting. At that same meeting the Consulting Firm provides the Client with a template for the Future State that's been populated with the opportunities found so far.

- **Complete Future State Vision**

The Vision includes a description of the future state human capital, processes, and tools.

- **Human Capital:** This is a set of intentions for the desired future state and should include a description of full human capital lifecycle and how it will be managed. Components include: job descriptions and standards, recruiting, hiring, compensation, on-boarding, payroll, training, evaluating, promoting, standards of conduct, and off-boarding.
- **Processes:** This is a set of intentions for the desired future state for the processes required in the organization and how they function both within and

between the organization's functional areas.

- **Tools:** A description of the tools necessary to operate the business in the future state. It should include the organization's Management Operating System, automated systems, and tooling required to complete the product lifecycle.

The future state evolves over the course of several days as the consulting team works with each executive to refine their input and resolve inconsistenties between the executives. Once there is alignment the Executive Team meets, reviews, and approves the future state.

- **Develop the Plan and Complete the Cost/Benefit Analysis**

The consulting team works with the organization to complete a gap analysis between the Current State and Future state showing the work that needs to be done to get from where they are to where they want to be. The plan is the set of activities that must be completed and, based on the goal, the resources, both internally and externally necessary to reach the stated goal by the stated date.

The cost is typically associated with increased labor, both internal and external, as well as any additional investment. The benefit is stated in terms of increased earnings before tax, depreciation, and interest. Both are stated over time.

Once completed and pre-briefed with the key executives, the Executive Team meets to discuss the plan together and decide upon the need for and timing of outside assistance. If needed, an offer letter is prepared and signed and the engagement is scheduled.

- **Deliver/Receive Payment**

The final invoice for the analysis is presented and paid.

Exercise II-11: Define Your Order to Cash Process and Describe Each Step

Step 1: | Step 2: | Step 3: | Step 4: | Step 5:

SECTION III: SET YOUR BUSINESS UP FOR SUCCESS

STEP 1: ESTABLISH YOUR BUSINESS

BUSINESS NAME

There are both legal and marketing ramifications to the name you choose for your business.

Because each state has its own rules depending upon the business structure, I recommend going to the Small Business Administration's website (sba.gov) and clicking on the link for your state to find out exactly what you need to do. (NOTE: sba.**com** is a business, not the government website.)

Legal Ramifications

If you are going to name your business anything but your surname, you'll need to register that name. This process of operating under your business' assumed name is called, 'doing business as', often abbreviated as DBA.

In the early days of your business, and before you incur expenses investing in marketing materials, it's important to register the name you've selected with your local government. As part of the registration process you'll not only confirm that no one else has selected that name but also protect that name so no one else can use it.

One method of determining whether your business name has been selected is to do an Internet search to see if there's anyone operating under that name. If you're going to be doing business on the Internet, you'll also want to ensure no one has purchased that URL or is operating a website under that name. You can do this by typing www.xxxxx.com into your web browser where the xxxxx is the name you want to use for your business.

Marketing Ramifications

Consider how many times you've done business with a company but can't remember their name. Selecting a name requires careful consideration and a bit of research. When selecting the name for your business consider that:

- The name of your business should indicate what your business is or does.
- It should be easy to say. One way of determining if it meets this criterion is to pretend you're answering the telephone with the name of your business ten times.
- It should be easy to remember.
- It shouldn't be easily misinterpreted to mean something else.
- It shouldn't limit your future business growth.

Exercise III-1: Select the Name for Your New Business:

____

SELECT A LEGAL STRUCTURE FOR YOUR BUSINESS

I recommend when you initially start your business, you start it as a sole proprietorship or if you have a partner, a partnership. This significantly reduces the start-up costs, simplifies the paperwork and accounting, and allows you to focus on whether this is a business you really want to operate. Having offered this suggestion, I have included a description of the different business legal structures.

Sole Proprietorship: Most small businesses are sole proprietorships. This is because:

- This is the least complex and least expensive to set up and operate.
- You alone are entitled to all profits and responsible for all debts.
- You don't have to take any action to establish this business as a legal entity if you operate under your own name.
- If you want to select a name for the business, you should file a DBA (doing business as) name with your local government.
- The biggest risk of organizing as a sole proprietorship is that your personal assets are not protected if you are sued.
- **Proprietorship Taxes**
    - Business income and expenses are calculated and entered on Schedule C and reported and filed with your 1040. In some cases, the business can file a schedule C-EZ.
    - Sole proprietors are not treated as employees. They must project how much they will earn for the year and make quarterly tax payments to avoid the estimated tax penalty. These payments cover not only income tax, but Social Security and Medicare as well.
- **Employees** Sole proprietorships can have employees. If so they must, like all businesses:
    - Report federal payroll tax information and make federal payroll tax deposits.
    - Report and pay annual federal unemployment tax.
    - Report annual wages for employees, and annual payments to contractors.

Partnerships

- At least two people are required to establish a partnership.

- There are two types of partnerships: general partnerships and limited partnerships; however, every partnership requires at least one general partner who is personally responsible for the debts and liabilities of the firm.

- Partnerships must file federal and state tax returns. The partners each must also file a schedule K-1 and pay any amounts owed for their personal taxes.

- **General Partnership**

  - Although a verbal agreement is said to be binding, it is strongly recommended to have a written partnership agreement that spells out the roles, responsibilities, powers, and authority of each partner.

  - This agreement should be drawn up by an attorney and typically costs $1,000 – $5,000.

  - This type of partnership, even with a signed agreement, does not limit the liability of general partners if there is a problem with the business.

- **Limited Partnership**

  - Limited partners typically have no authority in the management of or responsibilities for the day to day operation of the business.

  - They are typically investors whose liability is limited to their capital contributions plus any profit generated during the time of their agreement.

Corporations

Organizing your business as a corporation is the most complex of the business structures to set up, but informs the business and banking world that you're here to stay. There are three types of corporate structures, each with benefits and drawbacks.

- **The C-Corporation**
  - ➢ Because a corporation is a separate legal entity, the assets and debts of the organization are also separate and taxed separately.
  - ➢ Corporations are owned by shareholders and operated by officers.
  - ➢ It's not unusual for a small business owner who organizes this way to hold the stock and perform all the roles during the early stages.
  - ➢ Since one of the benefits of this type of business structure is that it limits the liability of the owners, it is essential to operate the corporation as a separate entity.
  - ➢ Even if you are the only attendee – hold shareholder meetings on at least an annual basis and keep records of decisions made in those meetings.
  - ➢ Operate a separate bank account to pay all expenses and accept all payments attributable to the business with that account.
  - ➢ All taxes owed by the corporation are not limited in liability and must be paid even if the company declares bankruptcy.
  - ➢ The list of forms you must file, taxes you must pay, and deadlines vary according to the state and type of business you're in. You can go online to sba.gov and get a list for your location and type of business.

- Corporations can make some deductions associated with the operation of their business that other forms of business are not allowed to make; however, owners are taxed at both the corporate and personal level for their income.

- Here is a list of standard taxes the corporation will be responsible for filing and paying:

  - Federal taxes for a C-Corporation are reported on IRS Form 1120. Annual state taxes are typically prepared and filed at the same time and vary greatly from state to state.

  - Sales taxes must also be reported and paid to the state.

  - Quarterly payroll taxes must also be reported and paid.

  - Federal unemployment taxes, based on the corporation's history, must also be reported and paid.

  - Annual state franchise taxes protect the name of your business and are based upon the corporation's income. In many states the franchise tax form must be filed regardless of whether the corporation makes a profit or has income if the business is open.

- **Subchapter S-Corporations**

  - This type of corporation requires that the company already be incorporated as a C-Corporation or a Limited Liability Corporation. The Subchapter-S is then elected using IRS form 2553.

  - There are circumstances when this election is not allowed, such as the method used the previous year for valuing inventory, the number and citizenship of shareholders, so check the rules carefully.

- Because some corporations make the switch to pass along higher start-up costs against personal income, it is difficult and not always possible to switch back from a Subchapter S-Corporation, so make this decision carefully.

- The benefit of organizing as a Subchapter S-Corporation is that it has the limited liability of a corporation but is taxed like a partnership.

- A Subchapter S-Corporation files its taxes using the same form as the C-Corporation, but then the corporation prepares a form K-1 for each shareholder according to their number of shares.

- Income or loss is then reported and paid on the shareholder's personal income taxes.

- **Limited Liability Corporations**
  - A Limited Liability Corporation, often referred to as the LLC, is a cross between a corporation and a partnership in that the business owners enjoy the limited liability of a corporation, but are taxed as a partnership.

  - The most significant benefit is that owners are not taxed twice on their personal income as they are with a Corporation.

  - The LLC is set up at the state level with the owners filing the articles of incorporation. The IRS considers this a state designation; therefore, the LLC must file its federal taxes as a Corporation.

  - There is no limit on the number of shareholders.

Exercise III-2: What business structure will you use to establish your business?

____

Why did you select this business structure?

____

REGISTERING YOUR BUSINESS

Registering your business name, or DBA, is done either with your county clerk's office or with your state government, depending on where your business is located. There are a few states that do not require the registering of business names.

Employer Identification Number (EIN)

An Employer ID (or EIN, for short) is a federal tax identification number for businesses. Although it's labeled as an identifier for "employers," you don't have to have employees to need an EIN. You can get one immediately by calling the IRS at 1-800-829-4933.

Permits and Licenses for Your Business for your business vary from state to state, county to county, and city to city. The www.sba.gov website will connect you to your state's website, so you can determine what permits and licenses you need by zip code and type of business.

Sales Tax Permit

Although I recommend you go to www.sba.gov, this is the one permit that's almost always needed if you're selling a product. Call the local sales and use tax office to determine if you need this permit if you are offering a service.

Exercise III-3: List the Federal, State, County, and Local Permits and Licenses you need for your Business, Where You Obtain Them, and your Plan for Obtaining them

____

____

____

____

____

____

____

STEP 2: SET UP YOUR BASIC BOOKKEEPING, TAX REPORTING, AND FINANCIAL RELATIONSHIPS

I used to believe that the earlier you could afford to hire a tax professional the better. My thinking has changed. The more you know and learn about the record keeping requirements and the federal, state, and local tax laws governing your business, the more a tax professional can help you.

Our government ensures business owners have access to all the information necessary to understand the required records to operate a business and pay business taxes.

The Small Business Administration has a full site of online courses available; therefore, this chapter is focused on ensuring you are aware of the topics you need to learn to set up your basic bookkeeping and financial relationships.

SET UP YOUR BASIC BOOKKEEPING

All money earned by the business is classified as **income** and everything spent by the business is an **expense**. The timing of income and expenses is know as **cashflow**. Just like the money you earn from a job (income), the bills you must pay (expenses) and the timing of money coming in and money going out (cashflow) there are some basics that will save you time and enhance your probability of success.

- Start with a plan of how you're going to keep a record of your business income and expenses and make the time to do it on a regular basis.

- Develop a process for filing your receipts so they're not in a shoebox. This offsets the time either you or your accountant will spend preparing your taxes and increases the probability that you'll remember everything.

- When your business earns income and pays expenses, do it from your business bank account. Don't co-mingle the money with your personal funds. If you need to make a loan to your business, write a check from your personal account to the business account, annotate it as a loan, and deposit it into the business account.

- For recurring expenses or equipment that are for both business and personal use, such as your cellphone (if you don't have a dedicated number for your business) or Internet, do the following:

    - Pay the expense from either your personal or business account.
    - Estimate the percentage of the expense related to personal and business use (should total 100%) and calculate the dollar value of that amount.
    - Reimburse your other account with that dollar amount.
    - Keep a record of these transactions.
    - For a vehicle that's for both personal and business use, record the number of miles driven for business, and use the current government mileage rate to reimburse yourself. The journal you use to record this should have the date, starting and ending destination, odometer readings, and mileage for each trip.

Categorize Expenses:

Because different types of income are taxed differently and most of the expenses you incur for your business are tax deductible you will want to have a categorized record of your income and expenses.

One method of doing this is to assign a three-digit code to each expense when it's made. You can use your check register, a simple spreadsheet, or accounting software to record and categorize expenses.

This list of codes is referred to as your **chart of accounts**. Because different categories of expenses have different tax rules, getting into this habit early can save you time later and reduce the probability that you will overlook a deduction.

As an example, here is a list of commonly used codes. You can use these, get a list from a book, or make up your own. What's important is to categorize your expenses so you can report them to the IRS and claim the deductions your business is entitled to claim.

- **BCH:** Bank Charge
- **CHA:** Business charitable contributions – be certain the contribution is to a registered charity and you have the receipt.
- **COM**: Communications expenses such as cell phone, land line, and Internet.
- **EQU**: Equipment purchased specifically for the business. If the equipment will be used for more than one tax year, deductions will typically be spread out over several years in the form of depreciation.
- **INV**: Inventory or items you use to make or package what you sell if you are selling a product.
- **INS**: Business insurance premiums.
- **OFC**: Expendable office supplies.
- **MAR**: Marketing expenses.

- **MIL:** Mileage expenses.
- **PAY:** Payroll expenses including salaries and withholding.
- **REF:** Reference materials and periodicals you need for your business.
- **REN:** Rental expense.
- **TAX:** Business taxes paid.

Categorize Income:

Because most of the income you receive from your business is either taxable or taxes you are collecting, you will also want to categorize your income.

- **INT:** Interest Income.
- **REV:** Revenue from sales or services.
- **TXC:** Tax collected from sales.

The record keeping you do for this depends upon whether you do a lot of small transactions or a few large transactions.

What's important is to ensure there's an audit trail from your sales to the money deposited. If there are a lot of small transactions, prepare a daily or weekly sales report and tie them to specific bank deposits. If there are a few large transactions, tie the invoices to specific bank deposits.

Monitor Your Cash Flow

The typical business incurs expenses prior to opening a bank account. Keep track of these expenses so you can reimburse yourself once your business starts to make money. Once you've registered your business and obtained your Tax Id open your bank account and keep track of your cash flow using your bank account ledger. Your bank account ledger is a chronological record of your deposits, withdrawals, and the remaining balance in your account.

The bank account ledger for Holiday Florists, below, shows an example of the transactions for their business start-up and first campaign.

HOLIDAY FLORISTS CHECK REGISTER

LEGEND

DC=Debit Card	AP = Automatic Payment
ATM=Automated Teller	BP = Online Bill Pay
DEP=Deposit	RE = Expense Reimbursement

DATE	ACTION	TRANSACTION	DESCRIPTION	CAT	WITHDRAWAL	DEPOSIT	BALANCE
12/6/2018	DEP	OPENING BALANCE	OWNER'S EQUITY	DEP		$500.00	$500.00
12/8/2018	DC	STAPLES	BUSINESS CARDS, INK, PAPER FOR FLYERS	OFC	$86.00		$414.00
12/10/2018	DEP	CASH PAYMENTS FROM SALES	WINTER HOLIDAY SALES	REV		$826.00	$1,240.00
12/10/2018	TXC	TAX COLLECTIONS FROM SALES	SALES TAX RATE .0825	TAX		$68.15	$1,308.15
12/17/2018	DC	FLORAL SUPPLIERS, INC	NON-PERISHABLE MATERIALS FOR HOLIDAY ARRANGEMENTS	INV	$234.00		$1,074.15
12/17/2018	DC	WHOLESALE FLOWERS, INC	FLOWERS FOR HOLIDAY ARRANGEMENTS	INV	$327.00		$747.15
12/20/2018	RE	OWNER REIMBURSEMENT	REIMBURSEMENT FOR MILEAGE 140 MILES * $.55	MIL	$77.00		$670.15
12/22/2018	AP	BANK FEE	BANK CHARGE FOR FIRST MONTH	BCH	$30.00		$640.15

In this example the business owner personally invested $500 to establish the business bank account and conduct the first sales campaign. He spent $86 to print business cards and brochures to promote the first campaign. As a result, had collected $826 and $68.15 in sales tax when he took customers' orders. He spent $234 on non-perishable items and $327 on the flowers. He drove 140 miles taking orders, buying what he needed to produce them, and delivering the finished bouquet. As a result, he made more than a 25% return on investment – quite successful for a first campaign.

Exercise III-4: Set Up Your Bank Account Ledger. In exercise II-11 you estimated your start-up costs. Use the worksheet below to complete an example of your bank ledger for your first campaign or sales event.

BUSINESS NAME:

LEGEND

DC=Debit Card	AP = Automatic Payment
ATM=Automated Teller	BP = Online Bill Pay
DEP=Deposit	RE = Expense Reimbursement

DATE	ACTION	TRANSACTION	DESCRIPTION	CAT	WITHDRAWAL	DEPOSIT	BALANCE

SET UP YOUR INVENTORY MANAGEMENT SYSTEM

If you're starting a business that sells products you make or buy, setting up an inventory management process is key because:

- It's essential to understand your Cost of Goods Sold (COGS), which is the value of all the ingredients or components and the packaging of each item you sell.

- It's important to know the value of the items in your inventory. If you spent $1,000 on non-perishable inventory and used half the items purchased, you still have $500 in inventory – IF all the items were purchased at the same price.

- If your product is made up of ten components with each purchased separately, you must know what you still have on-hand, so you know what you need to buy, and for tax reporting at the end of your business year.

- You need to consider the shelf life of your inventory and how fast the inventory 'turns' so you don't invest money in inventory that will expire before you can use or sell it.

There are many free or inexpensive tools available you can use to set up and manage your inventory. You can find these through a simple Internet search.

UNDERSTAND YOUR BASIC TAX OBLIGATIONS.

If your business makes a profit during the current tax year, you might need to pay taxes. If you're a sole proprietor, it will depend on your other income for the year, among other things.

If your business had a loss you might not need to pay taxes; however, documenting that loss is required and can offset other income or profits in future years.

If you are a sole proprietorship, you are self-employed and don't have taxes withheld from a paycheck; therefore, you are required to make estimated quarterly payments using form 1040-ES.

Sales Tax laws vary greatly by state, county, and local taxing authority. You collect sales tax from your customers, report it, and send it to the appropriate taxing authority.

Federal Taxes: In the Resources section below, I have listed some of the basic IRS documents you should read and understand. These are free to you on the government website www.irs.gov.

State, County, and Local Taxes: It would be so simple if every state, county, and local government had the same tax code. Since they don't, the website www.usa.gov provides a link to each state's government website. These websites typically have links to county websites, and the county websites usually have links to local government websites.

Exercise III-5: List the federal, state, county, and local tax obligations pertinent to your business and when they must be filed and paid:

____

____

____

____

____

____

ESTABLISH YOUR FINANCIAL RELATIONSHIPS

You will need to establish financial relationships with a bank and banking professionals, an accounting professional, a payment processor, and your suppliers.

Bank and Banking Professionals: New business owners typically establish their business account where they do their personal banking. While it's always wise to do business with organizations and people you know and trust, ensure your bank has a small business specialist, services and accounts with options favorable to a business. If not, your local chamber of commerce can often provide you with a list of banks who specialize in small business.

Once you've decided where to bank and have obtained your federal tax identification number, open a separate bank account for your business and put the start-up money you have in that account.

Payment Processors: Your selection of a payment processor is related to what type of business you're in. If you're in a business where people pay you using credit cards or through your website, you'll need an intermediary to process the payments.

Accounting Professionals: Once your business is making regular sales, and before you make your first payroll, you'll want to get advice from an accounting professional. You have options on what type to seek:

- **Certified Public Accountants (CPA):** Professionals who prepare taxes for submission, assess the financial viability of businesses, and advise.

- **Enrolled Agents:** Less expensive than a CPA, these are federally licensed tax practitioners who can perform many of the functions of a CPA, including preparing taxes and, if necessary, representing a taxpayer in front of the IRS.

- **Volunteer Income Tax Assistants (VITA):** Available through the IRS from mid-January through April for those with income of less than $51,000, they can help you prepare your taxes.

- **Small Business Administration (SBA):** The SBA has an army of volunteers through the SCORE program who can be assigned as mentors to help you with your questions.

Suppliers: Your suppliers are those you buy your products and supplies from. If you are producing and selling a product, have a business tax-id, and have established a relationship with a company who sells wholesale, you don't have to pay sales tax on items that are components of a product or those you will resell.

RESOURCES

- **Tax Savvy for Small Business,** F.W. Daily, 1997, NOLO Press Self-Help Law, Berkeley, CA.

- **Internal Revenue Service** (www.irs.gov):

    - IRS Publication 17: You're probably already familiar with this, as it governs Form 1040, the form you use to pay your personal taxes. If you've organized your business as a sole proprietorship, Schedule C is where you'll do much of your reporting, so pay attention to that section.
    - IRS Publication 334: Tax Guide for Small Business
    - IRS Publication 535: Business Expenses
    - IRS Publication 560: Retirement Plans for Small Business
    - IRS Publication 583: Starting a Business and Keeping Records

- **Government Agencies** (www.usa.gov): This website provides a link to every state government website as well as every federal agency.

- **Accounting Software:**

- **Microsoft Office** (www.office.microsoft.com): If you are already using Microsoft Office you can download many free Excel templates and tools to assist with your accounting.
- **Accounting Software** (http://accounting-software-reviews.toptenreviews.com) lists the following top suites of low cost accounting software.
- **Account Edge** (www.accountedge.com): Accounting software that has a 30-day free trial or a $99 one-time cost.
- **Freebooks** (www.freebooks.com): Accounting software with a 30-day free trial. A cloud accounting product that includes: invoices, expenses, time tracking, and reports. It's advertised to work with QuickBooks which can be an advantage as that's what many accountants use.
- **Quickbooks online** (www.quickbooks.intuit.com): Accounting software with a 30-day free trial. Multiple products are available and are priced from $12.95 to $39.95 per month.
- **Sage One** (www.na.sage.com): Accounting software that is advertised as a QuickBooks replacement, with options starting at $14 per month.
- **Xero** (www.xero.com): Accounting software that is advertised as a QuickBooks alternative. It has a 30-day free trial and is priced from $9 to $70 per month.
- **Zoho** (www.zoho.com): Accounting software that has a 14-day free trial and is $24 per month.

- **Inventory Management Software:** Many accounting packages include embedded inventory management software. There are also many standalone options including:

  - **Microsoft Office** (www.office.microsoft.com): If you are already using Microsoft Office, you can download many free templates and tools to manage your inventory.
  - **Bright Pearl** (www.brightpearl.com): Inventory management software for retailers that comes with a free trial.
  - **Skyware Inventory** (www.skywareinventory.com): Inventory management software that is free for one person, and $10 a month for each additional license.

STEP 3: SET UP YOUR BACK OFFICE

Your back office is everything you need to operate your business on a recurring basis. It includes:

- Information about your business.
- The management operating system that describes the process you use to plan, do, and review your business.
- The standard procedures you use to operate your business, train, and onboard your employees.
- The forms you need to support your workflow.
- The marketing materials you'll need to attract and retain customers.

BUSINESS INFORMATION

This is the collection of all the information about your business that isn't related to a process. It includes the business' name, address, telephone number, tax identification number and operating hours. It includes the URL for the website, the email address, and the passwords associated with these accounts.

It also includes the information repository of everyone related to your business including customers, employees, suppliers, and creditors.

It includes your business plan that contains:

- A brief Business Description of the business that anyone working for the business knows and uses when they describe the business and the business' vision and mission statement
- Professional Bios of you and anyone affiliated with your business.
- Competitive Analysis of businesses operating in your market.
- A marketing Plan for your products and/or services.
- A prototype Description of each of your products or services.
- An operating Plan that explains how you plan to operate your business.
- A financial Plan that explains how you manage finances of your business.

When you first start your business, everything relating to it typically fits in one hanging file or electronic folder. You'll be amazed how quickly the information multiplies. Setting up a file structure for that information and filing as you go can make the difference between your business succeeding or failing.

MANAGEMENT OPERATING SYSTEM

Your management operating system is the tool you use to establish the cadence for your company. It's an iterative process that should be relatively simple and straightforward when you start out.

When you developed the financial portion of your business plan you determined how much of your start-up funding you could afford to invest in your starting inventory or services. At the end of each cycle of delivery during your first year, **REVIEW** the results, what you did, how you did it, the results, and **PLAN** how you will **DO** the next cycle.

- **Review:** Describe the metrics (measures) that you'll use to evaluate your results.
- **Plan:** Based on your results, develop your plan for the next cycle.

- **Do:** Based on your results what can you do more efficiently or effectively?

Example 1-Product: Holiday Florists Mother's Day Campaign

- **Review:**

Cost of Goods Sold - Material: The goal for material costs to be less than 50% of total sales was achieved with the first campaign sales of $859.67 and material costs of $420.50.

Bouquet SKU	Sales Price Per Unit	Material Cost Per Unit	Profit Per Unit	Total Units Sold	Total Sales	Total Costs	Total Profit
M-1	$9.99	$4.50	$5.49	9	$89.91	$40.50	$49.41
M-2	$19.99	$11.00	$8.99	3	$59.97	$33.00	$26.97
M-3	$24.99	$12.00	$12.99	6	$149.94	$72.00	$77.94
M-4	$34.99	$17.00	$17.99	8	$279.92	$136.00	$143.92
M-5	$39.99	$19.00	$20.99	4	$159.96	$76.00	$83.96
M-6	$39.99	$21.00	$18.99	3	$119.97	$63.00	$56.97
TOTALS					$859.67	$420.50	$439.17

Cost of Goods Sold-Labor: Due to the learning curve associated with assembling each bouquet, time was collected during assembly of the final two units for each stock keeping unit (SKU). An hourly rate of $15.00 per hour was used for the metric, although the owner was not paid for her efforts.

Bouquet SKU	Sales Price Per Unit	Labor Cost Per Unit	Labor Profit Per Unit	Total Units Sold	Total Sales	Total Costs	Total Profit
M-1	$9.99	$2.50	$7.49	9	$89.91	$22.50	$67.41
M-2	$19.99	$7.50	$12.49	3	$59.97	$22.50	$37.47
M-3	$24.99	$5.00	$19.99	6	$149.94	$30.00	$119.94
M-4	$34.99	$5.00	$29.99	8	$279.92	$40.00	$239.92
M-5	$39.99	$7.50	$32.49	4	$159.96	$30.00	$129.96
M-6	$39.99	$10.00	$29.99	3	$119.97	$30.00	$89.97
TOTALS					$859.67	$175.00	$684.67

Total Cost of Goods Sold, Profit, and Contribution to Profit Margin: By looking at what the total costs would have been, had labor been paid, it's possible to determine what each SKU contributed to the profit margin. Going forward, labor and materials costs for all SKUs should be challenged.

Bouquet SKU	Sales Price Per Unit	Material Cost Per Unit	Labor Cost Per Unit	Profit Per Unit	Total Units Sold	Total Sales	Total Costs	Total Profit	Cont-ribution
M-1	$9.99	$4.50	$2.50	$2.99	9	$89.91	$63.00	$26.91	10%
M-2	$19.99	$11.00	$7.50	$1.49	3	$59.97	$55.50	$4.47	4%
M-3	$24.99	$12.00	$5.00	$7.99	6	$149.94	$102.00	$47.94	18%
M-4	$34.99	$17.00	$5.00	$12.99	8	$279.92	$176.00	$103.92	39%
M-5	$39.99	$19.00	$7.50	$13.49	4	$159.96	$106.00	$53.96	20%
M-6	$39.99	$21.00	$10.00	$8.99	3	$119.97	$93.00	$26.97	10%
TOTALS						$859.67	$595.50	$264.17	100%

- **Plan:** Fortunately, the Mother's Day campaign more than made back the cost of inventory. The next campaign is the graduation campaign. Since it happens so quickly following Mother's Day, many of the bouquet designs can be repurposed for graduation. The marketing approach for graduation is expanded to include displaying the prototype bouquets at the local Farmer's Market. A new brochure will need to be created. Once created it can be emailed to the customer list that expanded because of the Mother's Day orders.

- **Do:** The procedures used for the Mother's Day are reviewed and updated as needed, including the labor standards associated with each SKU.

Example 2-Service: Consulting Firm

- **Review:**

  The Pre-Analysis and Analysis sections of Analysis Management Operating System assessment was completed for the first analysis and shows improvement after each subsequent analysis.

Analysis Management Operating System			
ELEMENT	**DESCRIPTION**	**SCORE**	**COMMENT**
	Pre- Analysis Phase		
Goal	The client's goal is Specific, Measurable, Achievable, Relevant, and Time Based		
Goal Attainment	The client's executive team is aligned around the goal		There are several members of the decision network who are not aligned
Decision Network	The firm has confirmed the decision network for the Analysis and for any subsequent project		
Analysis Map	The Analysis Map has been reviewed with the Decision Network		Several members of the decision network did not attend the review meeting
Analysis Letter	The analysis letter clearly spells out each deliverable of the analysis, includes the client's responsibilities, and payment terms		Although the letter clearly spelled out the client's responsibilities the client needed to be reminded of these responsibilities
Scheduling	Prior to the analysis all meetings have been scheduled, calendared and participation has been confirmed with the key decision makers		
Data Request	All pertinent backgound information was requested and received prior to the start of the analysis		Much of the background was unavailable at the start of the Analysis
Pre-Analysis Communication	The Firm has provided the client with examples of announcement letters and the announcement letter has gone out to the whole company		
Logistics	All logistics including: safety, security, dress code, on-site hours, connectivity, printing, and work space have been confirmed prior to arrival		Safety requirements that include closed toed shoes in specific areas were not communicated prior to the start of the Analysis
Team Onboarding	The team has been recruited and completed the onboarding process		
Team Preparation and Training	The team has reviewed:all material provided by the client and all collateral prepared to date. Every team member has been trained on how to use every study template. The study templates and decks for the four meetings have been customized for the client. Hard copies of any templates (i.e., Executive Interview) necessary for note taking have been prepared		The four decks were not customized for the client prior to the start of the analysis
	Analysis Phase		
Kick-Off Meeting	All decision network members were present and participated in the kick-off meeting		
Current State-Executive Interviews	All executive interviews scheduled, conducted, and provided to the Analyst by noon Thursday of Week 1. All fields were completed, information met the criteria, and no templates were changed		25% of the executive interviews were not completed by noon Thursday. All were completed by team departure Friday of the first week
Current State-Process Flows	All functional area process flows were completed and provided to the Analyst by COB Thursday of Week 1 with a first-pass yield of >75%		
Current State-Management Operating Systems	Each consultant arrived the first day of the analysis with a drafted MOS for his/her functional area. The MOS was reviewed with the consultant's buddy and updated by COB the first day of the analysis. The completed MOS were provided to the Analyst prior to departure Friday of the first week		More that half of the MOS were not completed prior to arrival or complete with review by COB Monday
Current State-Area Study	Based upon the preliminary information that is assimilated a study is completed for each functional area		
Current State	The Analysis produced a clear understanding of the current state		There is not a clear understanding of the sales process
Future State Depiction	The Analysis Team produced a Future State Depiction in time for the Transition Meeting and provided the client with homework to review the meeting		
Future State	The client contributed to the Future State Depiction and produced a alignment on the future state		Although alignment was achieved n the Future State the client had minimal participation in the effort
Transition Meeting	All decision network members were present and actively participated in the Transition Meeting		
Implementation Plan	The Analysis Team produced the graphic of an implementation plan that broke out the work by functional team, depicted the work that needed to be done and in what order, showed a logical order of completion, and the specific deliverables that are required.		The level of detail and dependancies between workstreams was not complete in time for the Approach Meeting
Work Break Down Structure	Using the Implementation Plan, the Analysis Team produced a work break down structure that breaks the work down in executable tasks with the associated order and time for completion		The level of detail was too high to be executed
Charters	Using the Implementation Plan, the Analysis Team produced draft charters for each workstream		
Business Case	A business case is produced that shows at least a 5 to 2 cost to benefit ratio		
Approach Meeting	All decision network members were present and actively participated in the Approach Meeting		Two network members were absent due to business needs
Agreement Meeting	All decision network members were present, actively participated in the Leadership Alignment Meeting, and agreed to retain the consulting firm to assist with the implementation		

The firm was retained to assist with the implementation.

- **Plan:** Because the firm was retained to support the client during implementation the full team will be required during the engagement. This will require using delivery tools project leadership has used in the past and adhoc training for the team. As a result, there is no one available to fill the sales pipeline. At the end of this engagement the firm needs to address this by partnering with other small local firms for sales support.
- **Do:** Develop the delivery collateral. Update the consultants Analysis training to address the specific issues.

STANDARD OPERATING PROCESSES AND PROCEDURES

Your standard operating procedures are the collection of the processes and procedures you use to run your business. Often, owners of new business start-ups don't develop their standard operating procedures during their set-up phase because they are doing everything themselves while learning to do each step as they go.

Deferring this step until the business is up and running can add risk if a step is left out. If you defer this step and your business takes off it will be difficult to hire, onboard, and train anyone who can help you.

Standard Back Office Procedures Every business has processes and procedures they use to manage their business. Defining and following these processes helps you to perform them efficiently and at the right time. Some common processes businesses need to define are:

- **Customer Order Management:** This includes the procedure you'll follow when you take a customer order, including what information you'll collect, how you'll process the order, and where and how you'll store the information.
- **Customer Relationship Management:** This includes all the processes and procedures you'll follow throughout the customer lifecycle, including where, when, and how you'll store the information for each customer and their purchases.

- **Supplier Management:** This includes all the processes and procedures necessary to manage your suppliers.

- **New Product/Service Development:** This includes all the processes and procedures you'll follow to develop a new product or service.

- **Human Resource Management:** This includes all the processes and procedures you'll follow to manage your employees such as onboarding, training, payroll, benefits, and job descriptions.

- **Communications Management:** This includes the processes and procedures you use to communicate with your employees, investors, suppliers, and customers.

SECTION IV: SET YOURSELF UP FOR SUCCESS

STEP 1: YOUR PERSONAL FINANCES

Most of the businesses you'll be able to start for less than $1,000 won't yield enough return on investment the first year or two to be your primary means of support. To reduce the risk, it's essential to be able to satisfy your personal financial commitments without depending on income from your new business.

Analyze Your Monthly Financial Obligations

If you haven't calculated the amount of all your monthly financial obligations, this is a good place to start. List everything you owe or pay monthly, then take the time to analyze each expense and see if you have an opportunity to reduce it.

Be sure to include:

- **Housing:** The amount you spend is your choice but is largely dictated by the cost of living in your zip code and whether you live alone or with others who share the expense.

  If you're renting this is rent. When you own your own place you typically have a mortgage and may have a homeowner's association fee. You'll also pay property tax and will need to have money set aside for home repairs and improvements.

- **Utilities:** Your water and electricity can, to some extent, be opportunities to keep a little more of your hard-earned money in your pocket.

  - **Water:** If you live in an apartment that doesn't have a separate water meter you're going to pay a percentage of the overall bill. If, however, you get a bill that comes in your name or you live in a house, you can typically shave 10% off the bill just by not running water frivolously.

  - **Electricity:** Typically, the biggest portion of your electricity bill is from your heat in the winter and your air conditioning in the summer. You can, with a little effort, shave at least 15% off your bill every month by turning your thermostat down a few degrees in the winter or up a few degrees in the summer, changing your furnace filter, keeping your dryer vent clean, or investing in a ceiling fan. (In the winter set it to push the hot air back down and, in the summer, set it to pull the cool air up from the floor.)

- **Renter's or Homeowner's Insurance:** This is typically required if you're renting and essential if you're a homeowner. The basic cost of this insurance is based on the value of the property being insured and your credit score. Shop around. Rates can vary by as much as 200%.

- **Car Insurance:** The amount you pay for car insurance isn't just based on the value of your car and your driving record. If you've borrowed to buy the car and are still paying the loan, you must pay for full coverage which typically doubles the cost of your monthly insurance premium. The amount you pay is also based upon your credit score.

- **Health Insurance:** The next category of expenses is health insurance. As of now, our current administration is working to repeal the Affordable Care Act which requires all Americans to have health insurance. Regardless of your political leanings, when our government backs up their political beliefs with laws we need to understand the financial and medical implications.

If you don't have an employer-sponsored health care plan and you haven't purchased health care insurance, you won't have access to preventive care. This means you're rolling the dice and hoping you won't get sick and need medical care. If you do, you'll be seeking care with a "doc in the box" or, worse yet, at an emergency room. The team that treats you will assess the specific problem, treat that only, and you'll be presented with a whopping big bill.

- **Phone:** It's become a fact of life that we're tethered to our phones, but that doesn't mean this is a category of expense we can't reduce over time if we invest a little time in some activities to prevent us from needing to spend even more than our monthly plan.

  - **Prevent a Loss:** Most smart phones have a "find my phone" application. The kicker is that if you lose your phone and haven't set up this app before that happens, it's too late. Take the time to download the app and set it up now before this happens. You'll also have to set up the app on another device such as an iPad or computer, so you can use that device to find the phone. Another option is to set up "Family Sharing" so that someone you designate can "see" where your phone is.

  - **Change Providers or Plans:** When your next statement comes look at the charges. Are you using what you're paying for? Are you paying extra charges? Is your current phone or plan eligible for an upgrade? After reviewing this information, compare mobile plans in your area. If you find one that's less, call your current provider and find out how to lower your rates. If they don't offer that, let them know you'll call them back. Then call the lower-cost provider and determine if there are any other charges to switch.

  - **Hanging onto or Upgrading Your Cellphone:** If your account indicates that you're eligible for an upgrade, it typically means you have completed making payments on your phone and your monthly bill should have been reduced. If that didn't happen and this is the first month you've been eligible, call them and find out if it will be reduced and by how much.

Phones today are ridiculously expensive, particularly when you choose to upgrade to the next model. The companies producing phones are marketing geniuses and work hard to convince you that upgrading is essential. (You don't have the new features now and you're getting along fine, right?) So, this might be an opportunity to reduce your monthly expenses.

- **Internet/Wifi/TV:** The options here are endless and continue to change, and which carriers and plans are available vary by location. Basic Internet and Wifi can be purchased relatively inexpensively, often for less than $40 per month. It goes without saying that the costs go up as you add capability and services. There are plenty of articles online that discuss ways to reduce your TV bill.

- **Car Note:** One of your goals should be to pay off your car note early. Regardless of the interest rate, if you have a car note with anything more than zero interest, you are paying more for the vehicle than it's worth.

- **Credit Card Debt:** Credit cards are wonderful tools to buy what you want when you want or need something. Let's say that new sofa you *had* to buy because it was on sale is now at full price or more; if you put it on your credit card and didn't pay it off when the payment was due you're literally throwing money in the garbage.

  Having said that, it's tough to do business today without a credit card. Find one with no annual fee that gives you cash back on purchases and use it for groceries, gas, and incidentals and pay it off every month. You'll earn a little bit of money and it will boost your credit score.

- **Savings:** This is a critical category of expense. If you don't budget for it and sock it away every month, you might be one emergency away from disaster. These disasters show up in many forms and by not saving you're inviting them. For example, if you don't put away money for your taxes, you can end up owing the IRS and paying a fine. If you don't get your oil changed on a regular basis, your car won't last as long, and you might end up with expensive repairs before you've even paid it off. An unreliable car can cause you to show up late for work too many times, get you fired, and put you at risk to not be able to pay next month's rent.

Your savings should be split between short-term, which includes emergency funds, and long-term savings. Each has a different purpose.

Your emergency fund should be your starting point. This is the fund that's going to prevent one of the disasters I just mentioned from making you broke while allowing you to remain financially stable. It should contain two months of living expenses. This allows you to go to the dentist when you should instead of waiting until you have a cavity. It pays for an unexpected car repair, a plumber, or a repair to your cell phone. When we take money out of our emergency fund it needs to be replaced ASAP.

Your short-term savings allow you to make wise short-term decisions and you can start saving just as soon as you've put enough away for your emergency fund. This is where you start to get ahead of the game. When you start out, your short-term savings is an account where you put the funds you plan to spend on one-time expenses over the next year. This pays for your contact lenses, your tune-up or new tires, your annual medical deductible, the down payment on a new car, and Christmas.

When you really start to accumulate a balance in your short-term savings account you give yourself the opportunity to be able to afford to start a business.

Your long-term savings is for your future. The need to save for this is more important than ever before. Gone are the days when we could expect to receive a pension from an employer that would support us in our old age.

Depending upon your age, relying on Social Security is also a risk. Unexpected expenses or routine price increases in products and services typically outpace Social Security's cost of living increases.

We all know we need to start saving now, however, more than 50% of American families have no retirement savings. What we're giving up is our future financial stability.

This all sounds like "blah, blah, blah" if you're short every month just paying the bills.

We'll address that shortly. The point to understand is that savings is an essential category of expense and should be included when adding up your monthly expenses.

- **Discretionary Spending:** Your discretionary spending includes what you spend each month for food, gas, shoes, toothpaste, haircuts, clothes, drinks after work, and even kitty litter. Depending upon what you're spending, this is often the category with the biggest opportunity to save money. By understanding what you're currently spending, you can establish a specific amount you're going to spend each week and stick to it.

Exercise IV-1: Set an Amount You're Going to Spend this Week; Track Your Spending; Analyze the Results:

____

____

____

____

____

Exercise IV-2: What Opportunities Do You Have to Reduce Your Current Expenses?

____

____

____

____

____

Analyze Your Monthly Income: Add together any sources of income you have.

- **Salary:** If you're paid a salary use the net amount. If you're paid on an hourly basis use the average number of hours per month plus the average amount of overtime you typically earn. If you're paid by the shift and the amount is variable, estimate your monthly earnings.

  Clearly, you're thinking of starting your own business or you wouldn't be doing this course. If you're currently employed it is essential to be the best employee you can possibly be right now. The professionalism you demonstrate every day will determine whether the people you're working with now will be your customers in the future.

Make certain your job performance is stellar. This includes being on time every day, having a great attitude no matter what, not criticizing your boss or the owners, and being a good teammate. Believe me, I know it can be tough when you're making plans to start your own business, but it is essential, and being appreciative of the people currently providing your current income never hurts.

If this is not what you've been doing, change your performance now. You'll be surprised how quickly the change will be noticed. Wait until your boss comments on the change (to you or someone else), then admit you recognized you could do better and made the change.

Exercise IV-3: What Opportunities Do You Have to Improve Your Current Performance or Increase Your Value to Your Employer?

____

____

____

____

____

- **Social Security:** If you're collecting social security use the net amount. It's also a good idea to figure out how much income you can earn before it starts to affect your monthly payment. You can find that information online at www.ssa.gov.

- **Pension or Retirement:** Add to your income any monthly pension or retirement you might be receiving.

- **Unemployment or Other Benefits:** If you're currently unemployed or receiving other benefits, include those with the understanding that you may be required to look for and accept work you are offered.

Exercise IV-4: Do the Math:

My Monthly Income: ____________

My Monthly Expenses: ____________

Difference: ____________

Now that you know what your monthly numbers are, monitor your income and expenses against them on a weekly basis so you can adjust what you're doing to be able to meet these numbers.

Subtract your monthly living expenses from your monthly income. It comes down to simple math. If what you have coming in doesn't equal what you have going out, you need to do something about it. You can reduce your monthly expenses, get a part-time job or develop an alternate source of income that could potentially become a business start-up.

Close the Financial Gap

If you need an additional or an alternate source of income to meet your monthly financial obligations or to fund a business, your starting point needs to be either a part-time job or a product or service you're capable of providing with very little financial investment.

If you decide to get a part-time job, consider taking one working in the type of business you want to start. It will give you an opportunity to learn about the business you want to start and determine whether you'd really be happy owning and operating that type of business.

If you can't find something part-time in the type of business you want to start, consider a part-time job in the type of venue where your products or services will be sold.

You can also consider working part-time in a business that attracts customers in your target market.

Next, review your current schedule to determine what hours you have available to earn additional income. A word of caution: don't make the mistake I've made of trying to work seven days a week to make that number. Even when you're not making your number, if you try to do this, in the long term you end up neglecting other parts of your life, not getting enough rest, and risking your health. That lifestyle eventually catches up to you, and you don't want to neglect something crucial.

Exercise IV-5: Complete the Availability Table with days and times you're available to earn additional income:

Days I'm Available	Times I'm Available

Once you have identified WHAT it is you want to do and WHEN you are available to do it, you can either look for a part-time job doing that OR look for customers.

There are many opportunities if you're willing to invest the time and take pride in your work. Let everyone you meet know you're available and when. You can have some inexpensive business cards printed with a list of services and your phone number to give out when someone shows interest. You'll be surprised how quickly you can build a steady clientele and an alternate source of income.

Exercise IV-6: What are the first three steps you should take and the dates you'll complete each step to get your first customer or find a part-time job?

	Action	Date
Step 1		
Step 2		
Step 3		

Why are you willing to commit to these actions by these dates?

____

____

____

____

____

If your alternate source of income starts to grow into a regular source of income, above $300 a year, you'll want to register your business. The Small Business Administration's Website at www.sba.gov provides a link to every state so you can find out exactly how and where to do that.

STEP 2: YOUR TIME

Time is an equal opportunity employer. Each human being has the same number of hours and minutes every day. Rich people can't buy more hours. Scientists can't invent new minutes. And you can't save time to spend on another day. Even so, time is amazingly fair and forgiving. No matter how much time you've wasted in the past, you still have an entire tomorrow.

~Denis Waitley

Manage How You Spend Your Time

I've often heard it said, "Work will expand to take up the available time." That's true regardless of whether you're working full-time for someone else, starting a new business or running a company. Until you consciously decide how you're going to spend your time you'll probably never have enough of it and always feel as if you're behind.

The key word is "consciously". We each get 24 hours a day, seven days a week, for a total of 168 hours a week. No more, no less. To function effectively we need to carve out time for our work and/or business while ensuring we set aside time to sleep, eat, exercise, shower, pay bills, relax, and connect with our friends and families.

Exercise IV-7: Analyze How You Currently Spend Your Time: For the next seven days, before you go to bed, plan how you're going to spend each hour of the following day starting with the time you're going to wake up. Each day keep a record of how you spent your time throughout the day, along with any interruptions and comments regarding whether you were on task. At the end of the day, before you go to bed, record your observations, then plan for the following day. You can use a journal, one of the many free time management apps, or the charts provided.

Day 1: ________

Time	Planned Activities	Actual Activities	Interruptions	Comments

Observations/Opportunities:

Day 2: ________

Time	Planned Activities	Actual Activities	Interruptions	Comments

Observations/Opportunities::

____

____

Day 3: ________

Time	Planned Activities	Actual Activities	Interruptions	Comments

Observations/Opportunities::

____

____

Day 4: ________

Time	Planned Activities	Actual Activities	Interruptions	Comments

Observations/Opportunities::

____

____

Day 5: ________

Time	Planned Activities	Actual Activities	Interruptions	Comments

Observations/Opportunities::

Day 6: ________

Time	Planned Activities	Actual Activities	Interruptions	Comments

Observations/Opportunities::

____

____

Day 7: ________

Time	Planned Activities	Actual Activities	Interruptions	Comments

Observations/Opportunities::

____

____

Exercise IV-8: What are the Changes You Need to and are Willing to Make?

____

____

____

Taking control of how you spend your time is empowering. Now that you've analyzed the changes you want to make and committed to making them, set yourself up for success by making your plan for tomorrow at the end of each day.

Plan What You'll Do Tomorrow Before You Finish Today

One of the most effective methods for optimizing your activities is the tool used by Phil Maxwell, who, when I met him, was the Chief Information Officer (CIO) for Neiman Marcus. At a time in history when CIO typically stood for "Career Is Over", I met with him in his office and was astounded to see his office was not only pristine, but Phil was relaxed, on time for our meeting, and completely focused on our discussion.

Phil's department was implementing a new point of sale system as well as several other major initiatives. Just before our time was up I asked him how he managed to stay so organized and focused.

The method he shared with me has become a tool that not only increased my effectivity, it's something I've shared with dozens of executives and business owners and in turn have seen their effectiveness increase.

He simply scheduled the last meeting of each day as a meeting with himself and used that time to reflect on what he'd accomplished that day, prepare for the next day, and clean up anything he hadn't finished before leaving.

As a result, when he left work each day he had not only a sense of closure, but a plan for the next day. This allowed him to be present for his family or for whatever he was doing.

When you're starting a new business, this is tough because you may be carving out time from an already busy schedule. You can still take advantage of the Maxwell method by planning what you'll do at the end of the time you have available to work on each activity.

Exercise IV-9: Try the Maxwell Method. At the end of the day or at the end of the time you must work on an activity, plan what you'll do the next day or the next time you have scheduled to work on this activity.

Plan for Tomorrow:

____

____

____

____

____

____

____

____

____

STEP 3: SET UP YOUR PERSONAL BACK OFFICE

Establish a Paperwork Management System

Letting paper stack up is one of those "I'll get to it later" habits that can get you in trouble if you don't put in place a method of managing it. This applies to both your personal paperwork and the paperwork you'll accumulate when you start your new business.

One method of managing it is the folder system. You can do this even if you don't have a file cabinet by using a simple banker's box you can find at any office supply or big box store.

While you're there, pick up hanging folders in two colors, one for your business files and one for your personal files. I recommend choosing the type that come with plastic labels that include paper inserts that slide into the labels making it easy to label each one.

I've also found it helpful to have a personal folder and a business folder labeled "bills" where I can store unpaid bills until I pay them, a personal folder and a business folder labeled "action" where I can temporarily store everything I need to do, and a personal and a business folder labeled "information" where I can temporarily store any information I want to read.

You might also consider getting rid of the paper altogether by setting up electronic folders and digitizing incoming mail and important papers.

Exercise IV-10: Set up your Paperwork Management System: Collect the supplies you need, decide where you're going to store your "file cabinet", and label a folder for each type of document.

Tame the Paper and Electronic Tiger

If you're like most of us, just one hour of focused effort will get you started taming the paper tiger and reduce the stress associated with having unorganized stacks of paper laying around.

Exercise IV-11: Quick Start Exercise to Tame the Paper and Electronic Tiger

- **Step 1:** Set a timer for one hour.
- **Step 2:** Select a work area and be sure to have a trash can or shredder handy.
- **Step 3:** Gather up all your loose paper and periodicals and take them to your work area.
- **Step 4:** Get rid of everything you don't need:
    - Throw away the junk mail that's addressed to "occupant" or "resident" or to people who used to live there.
    - Throw away all the back issues of periodicals that have been stacking up.
- **Step 5:** File everything you can.
- **Step 6:** Put bills, items requiring action, and information you want to read later into their respective folders.
- **Step 7:** Open and sort your unopened mail or mail you haven't dealt with.

- **Step 8:** If you still have time left in the hour, take care of the most important actions until you run out of time.

- **Step 9:** If you haven't made a dent in the stack, schedule another hour later today or this week to work on it again.

Reduce Your Incoming Paper Mail

The previous exercise demonstrates how much you can get done in just one hour when you're focused. Reducing the amount of incoming information, whether it's paper or electronic, and managing the remainder as it's coming in optimizes the use of your time.

According to usa.gov/telemarketing you can take several actions to stop the delivery of unwanted mail in your mailbox:

Tell companies you do business with to remove your name from customer lists they rent or sell to other companies. Look for information on how to opt-out of marketing lists on sales materials, order forms, emails, and websites.

Contact the Data & Marketing Association to sign up for their mail preference service. This will allow you to remove your name from most national telemarketing, mail, and email lists. Register online for $2 or by completing and mailing the registration form.

The Consumer Credit Reporting Industry's Opt-Out Program lets you stop receiving credit card and insurance offers. All major credit reporting agencies (Equifax, Experian, Innovis, and TransUnion) participate in this program. Register online or call 1-888-567-8688 to opt-out of receiving these offers for five years.

If you have previously completed a request to opt-out from receiving firm (pre-screened and pre-approved) offers for credit or insurance, you must complete a request to opt-in to begin receiving offers again.

Opting-out will not end all mail solicitations. You may still receive mail from local merchants, religious and charitable organizations, professional and alumni associations, politicians, and companies with whom you do business.

Exercise IV-12: Reduce Your Incoming Mail

- **Example 1: You don't need this product or service:**

Street Address
City, State, Zip
Date

Addressee
Street Address
City, State, Zip

Dear Sir or Madam:

I acknowledge receipt of your latest correspondence and recognize the expense incurred in sending it.

I have no need for the product or service, but if that changes, I will contact you.

Please remove the undersigned from your mailing list.

Kind regards,

Your typed name
Your signature

- **Example 2: You'd prefer to receive mail electronically:**

Street Address
City, State, Zip
Date

Addressee
Street Address
City, State, Zip

Dear Sir or Madam:

I acknowledge receipt of your latest correspondence and recognize the expense incurred in sending it.

My email address is XXXX@XXX.

This is a written request that you send all correspondence electronically to that address.

Additionally, do not share my name or contact information with any other organizations. If I previously authorized that sharing, I immediately revoke that authorization and request you notify those organizations.

Kind regards,

Your typed name
Your signature

Exercise IV-13: Manage Your Paper: For the next week, pick up your mail every day.

- **Step 1: Open and Sort Your Mail.** Quickly sort all your mail (and any mail you didn't deal with during Exercise IV-11, Step 4) into four piles. Pile 1 is junk mail. Pile 2 is the stack of periodicals or items you want to read later that require no other action on your part. Pile 3 is information that came through the mail that you want to review such as sales advertisements. Pile 4 is mail addressed to you that you either recognize as requiring action or that you'll have to open to determine if it requires action.

  Now that your mail is in stacks it's easier and less time consuming to deal with.

- **Step 2: Get Rid of Pile 1.** Throw every piece of junk mail you don't want to read that doesn't have your name and address on it into the recycle bin. If your mailbox is outside and you can throw it a recycle bin before it enters your place, do it.

  If the mail has your name and address on it, either shred it or tear up the portion that includes your contact information small enough to require a lot of work to tape it back together. Identity theft is way too time consuming to deal with.

- **Step 3: Reduce Pile 2,** your stack of old periodicals. Take a hard look at what you've been saving. Is it worth the space you're giving it? Is the information available somewhere else? If so, get rid of it.

  If there's an article you really want to keep on a specific topic tear those pages out of the magazine and make a file for it, or, better yet scan it and save it as a PDF in an electronic folder.

- **Step 4: Sort the Mail Addressed to You.** Open each piece of mail and sort it into Bills, Action, and Information piles. (If you find any junk mail, rip it up or shred it.) Deal with anything that must be dealt with in less than a week, such as a bill that needs to be paid or a call that needs to be made. File everything in the file for that category or in the bills, actions, or information file.

Manage Your Email

The speed at which you answer your email is a determining factor in how much you get. Because of this, at some point, it will be important to have different email addresses for your personal and business email accounts.

Just as having stacks of paper all over the house wastes time when you're trying to find something and can cause you problems if you forget about it, the same applies to email.

Two types of inventory management, Last In, First Out (LIFO) and First In, First Out (FIFO) can be combined as a powerful tool to manage your email and clean out all the old email you have.

Exercise IV-14: Manage Your Email.

- **Step 1: Establish the Frequency, Times, and Duration for Checking Your Incoming email. Fill in the blanks.**

  I'm going to check my email ________________ times per day at the following times: ____. Each time I check my email I'm going to spend _______________________ minutes managing my inbox.

- **Step 2: Deal with the Junk Mail and Old Periodicals.** Scan down everything that arrived in your inbox. Delete all the junk mail and periodicals except for the one junk email that was the last to arrive (LIFO). Sort your email box so that everything that you've ever received from that sender is together. Delete every junk email you received except the last one. If you decide you no longer want to receiveemail from this sender, set up a "block" or unsubscribe from their mailing list.

- **Step 3: Review and answer urgent Email.** For the time remaining in this segment review and either respond to the remaining email that's arrived with the goal of responding to the most urgent. After responding to an email, delete it. (Your response remains in your outbox. You don't need to have it in both places.)

- **Step 4: End of Day.** Your goal for the last email segment of the day is to have responded to everything that required your attention today. If you received something that's going to take longer than the time available, move it to the Action folder you've established under your In-Box then add the action to your 'to do' list.

STEP 4: SET UP A PRIORITIZED "TO DO" LIST

Have you ever had the feeling of always being behind or that you can't possibly accomplish everything you need to do? Do you have tasks that, if completed, would simplify or improve your life, even if by just a little bit?

Most of us keep some form of "To Do" list; however, if you're anything like me, there are tasks that don't make the list that should have, tasks I put off because I don't enjoy (or dread) doing them, or tasks I leave until the last minute that I procrastinate about, resulting in consequences I could have avoided.

There are many methods for managing the things you need to do. For most of us, if we don't manage the list, it's easy to forget or put off doing something that ends up costing us time or money.

There are an abundance of templates and apps available online and through standard office products. You can also make your own template, use a journal, or simply a piece of paper. Be certain the tool you choose is easy for you to use.

Exercise IV-15: "To Do" List Quick Start: Set a timer for 1 hour.

- **Step 1: Make a list of everything you can think of you need to do.**

Category	Task	Scheduled	Completed
	Laundry		
	Get Car Inspected		
	Make Dental Appointment		
	Complete this week's Workbook Exercises		
	Exercise		
	Balance Checkbook with Bank Statement		
	Renew Driver's License		
	Clean Out Hall Closet		
	Find Handyman to Replace Cabinet		
	Buy Groceries		

- **Step 2: Categorize the List by Task Frequency**

Identify your recurring tasks. Start out with the tasks you need to do daily but often put aside because you run out of time. I don't typically put other daily things (Get up, eat breakfast, take shower) on the list. Next identify those you must do weekly (Laundry), then monthly (Balance Checkbook) to keep your life moving smoothly.

Category	Task	Scheduled	Status
D	**Exercise**		
W	**Laundry**		
W	**Complete this week's Workbook Exercises**		
W	**Buy Groceries**		
M	**Balance Checkbook with Bank Statement**		
	Get Car Inspected		
	Make Dental Appointment		

	Renew Driver's License		
	Clean Out Hall Closet		
	Find Handyman to Replace Cabinet		

Take a minute and look at your list. In the example, tasks such as clean house, pay bills, and run errands weren't listed. Often, we fail to list, and as a result, don't set aside time for some important tasks.

The remaining items on the list are those that are either non-recurring (Find Handyman to Replace Cabinet) or those done infrequently (Renew Driver's License).

- **Step 3: Prioritize the Non-Recurring or Infrequent Tasks on your List.**

The best method I've found is "The Eisenhower" method. Eisenhower commanded more than 2 million soldiers during World War II and developed this method of prioritizing his work.

Categorize each task on your 'to do' list based upon its importance and urgency and put it into the Eisenhower Box by answering the following: (graphic and explanation from www.thousandinsights.files.wordpress.com) Is this task important or not important and is this task urgent or not urgent?

	Urgent	Not Urgent
Important	Crying Baby Kitchen Fire Some Calls **DO** (1)	Exercise Vacation Planning **PLAN** (2)
Not Important	(3) Interruptions Distractions Other Calls **DELEGATE**	(4) Trivia Busy Work Time Wasters **DELEGATE**

Priority 1 tasks are tasks that are both urgent and important. These tasks need to be addressed personally and immediately. However, if you're spending most of your time on these tasks, you're just putting out fires. This is usually an indicator that you're merely reactive and are not managing your priorities and actions ahead of time.

Priority 2 tasks are tasks that are important but not urgent. These tasks need to be addressed personally but not immediately so they need to have a planned date or frequency if they're recurring tasks. Ideally, most of your tasks should be priority 2 tasks.

Priority 3 tasks are ones that are urgent but not important, so they require immediate attention, but not necessarily by you. These tasks are usually other people's priorities, not yours. If possible, delegate them, if not, move them to a Priority 4.

Priority 4 tasks are tasks that are neither urgent nor important, so they are mostly a waste of time. These tasks should be dropped as they provide little value, or taken off your To Do List and performed during your free time.

Category	Task	Scheduled	Status
D	**Exercise**		
W	**Laundry**		
W	**Complete this week's Workbook Exercises**		
W	**Buy Groceries**		
M	**Balance Checkbook with Bank Statement**		
1	**Get Car Inspected**		
2	**Make Dental Appointment**		
2	**Renew Driver's License**		
4	**Clean Out Hall Closet**		
3	**Find Handyman to Replace Cabinet**		

- **Step 4: Schedule Your Tasks:** By scheduling a day or date for each recurring task and a date for each non-recurring or infrequent task you're making a commitment to yourself to complete the task by a specific day of the week or month or on a specific date.

Category	Task	Scheduled	Status
D	Exercise	5 Days a week; Tues – Sat	
W	Laundry	Saturday	
W	Complete this week's Workbook Exercises	Saturday	
W	Buy Groceries	Thursday	
M	Balance Checkbook with Bank Statement	21st	
1	Get Car Inspected	8/15	
2	Make Dental Appointment	8/23	
2	Renew Driver's License	8/30	
4	Clean Out Hall Closet	9/7	
3	Find Handyman to Replace Cabinet	9/15	

- **Step 5: Manage Your List:** Throughout the day as items are completed you can cross them off the list or annotate the status column with a 'C'. When you add an item to the list, write it in at the bottom, annotating it with an 'A'.

  At the end of each day review what you've accomplished, schedule any tasks you've added, and put the tasks for the next day.

Exercise IV-16: Manage Your "To Do" List for a week.

- **Question 1: What did you learn about yourself?**

  ____

  ____

  ____

  ____

  ____

- **Question 2: What can you do to improve your effectiveness?**

____

____

____

____

____

STEP 5: CONDUCT A WEEKLY PERSONAL BUSINESS MEETING

Most successful businesses have a weekly meeting where results are reviewed and the next week is planned. The business of running a successful life is no different.

Setting one day a week to take care of the things that keep your life running smoothly significantly reduces your stress because it prevents the "emergencies" that happen when we didn't take the time to prevent them.

If you consider all the hours you spend doing one thing while worrying about something you're not doing, you understand what I mean. The luxury, and it might seem like a luxury, of taking a whole day off for yourself might be out of reach, but you can get there incrementally.

Set a Day and Time

Even if the first week you can only carve out an hour or two, set a day and time, then set an alarm for that time. I find that by not only setting the day, but also setting the time, I'm motivated to get out of bed, particularly on my day off when all I'd really like to do is sleep.

As weeks go on you'll find you have been sub-consciously preparing for your meeting all week.

Exercise IV-17: Set the day and start time for your first weekly business meeting:

____

Make Wise Use of This Time

Turn off the ringer and automatic notifications on your cellphone. To be effective you must be able to focus.

If you've got something that's urgent and important, do it first. Additionally, if there's something that can be going in the background - like washing a load of laundry or running the dishwasher – get it started and on auto-pilot.

It's important to manage your time during your "weekly meeting". You want to complete all three activities: meeting preparation, financial progress review, and taking action during the meeting time so you have some time for yourself.

- **Activity 1: Meeting Preparation** Get everything you're going to need in one, uncluttered place. Make sure you have an empty trash can to throw away everything you're going to discard and, if you recycle, a container for all the paper you'll be tossing.

  If you have mail that's come in since your initial sort, process it first so you can update and prioritize your "To Do" list and most current bills and action items.

  If your bank statement came in this week, either electronically or on paper, reconcile it with your budget. This allows you to make spending decisions based upon an accurate bank balance.

- **Activity 2: Financial Progress Review** This is the time to look forward while you have enough time to prevent getting into trouble. Determine where you are against where you need to be. Review your monthly budget, and if the month is more than half over, use next month's projection. Determine where you are against where you need to be for the next several weeks. Are you on track or do you need to spend more time during the next week to come generating additional or alternate income?

- **Activity 3: Take Action**

➢ **Pay your bills.** Pay the bills that need to be paid for the upcoming week and fund your weekly expenses.

➢ **Work down your "To Do" list.** First, take care of the urgent and important items on your "To Do" list. Next review the items that are important but will become urgent if you don't take care of them this week and take care of them.

➢ **Update your "To Do" list.** Take a minute or two to review what you accomplished (or should have) last week. Remove the items you accomplished, prioritize, and schedule the what you need to accomplish in the upcoming week.

I used to labor under the misperception that one magic day everything on my list would be done. I finally came to understand there would always be additional tasks to add to the list and that by not putting off the things I had to do and getting them done, I wouldn't have to spend time or money on damage control.

We've all been guilty of spending energy fabricating excuses about why we didn't complete something on time. Coming to the realization that getting something done on or ahead of schedule ensures you have time to do other things on your list and work on your new business sets you up for success.

➢ **Clean Your Space and Do Your Laundry:** Why, you might ask, is there a section during a weekly business meeting for cleaning your space? Because, time is money and it takes less time to keep a place clean if you do it every week than if you do it when it gets so bad you can't stand it.

It also takes less time to keep stuff well organized than it does to waste time looking for things you can't find or finding out you have no clean socks when you're getting ready for work or an important business meeting.

No one likes to come home to or wake up to a dirty place. Taking one hour a week to clean your place so the bathroom, kitchen, and bedroom are clean reduces stress and makes it easier to keep clean than it is to get it clean.

- **Run Your Errands:** Plan out the route you're going to take and set off to do all your errands in one trip. You'll find going to the bank, grocery store, and gas station once a week, rather than every day, helps your money go a lot further.

  Convenience stores co-located with gas stations typically charge quite a premium for grocery items. You pay a high cost for that "convenience".

  This is also your time to stop and get the pair of jeans, shoes, or new shirt you need. Establish a habit of buying what you need when you need it in weekly increments rather than going on a spending spree when you've had a great week.

Exercise IV-18: Conduct your first weekly business meeting, then answer the following questions:

- **Did I accomplish what I set out to accomplish?** ________________
- **What can I do between now and next week's business meeting to make this time even more productive?**

  ____

  ____

  ____

  ____

SECTION V: GET OUT OF YOUR OWN WAY

STEP 1: MAKE THE DECISION TO BE HAPPY

The day I realized happiness was a choice was a turning point in my life. I don't remember if I read it somewhere or if it was a line in a movie, but even if I'd heard it before, I finally understood it.

Until that moment I believed happiness was conditional. As in: I'll be happy ***when*** ________. (Fill in the blank: … my business is successful, I find true love, I lose ten pounds.) I had bought into the idea that the pursuit of happiness (as promised by the U.S. Constitution) meant realizing my dreams through hard work.

Exercise V-1: Do You Believe "Happiness is a Choice"?

____

____

____

____

After I made the decision to be happy I found the decision was the easy part. I had to learn how to be happy. For me that meant learning to live in the moment, to be grateful and thankful, and accepting and respecting other people for who they are and what they believe. In other words, I had to change.

Exercise V-2: Do You Know How to Be Happy or Is There More for You to Learn?

____

____

____

____

I made the decision to get up an hour earlier every day to read, write, and meditate. I started with a book recommended by a friend, which led to another, and another, and another. I read a little every day, write what I understand to be the lesson and what I'm grateful for. Then I spend a few minutes meditating.

Exercise V-3: Do You Want to Change Your Level of Happiness? If so, how will you go about making that change?

____

____

____

It's been many years since that day and, although I'm not yet the person I am meant to be, I'm better than I was, and I'm happy.

STEP 2: REPLACE NEGATIVE SELF-TALK WITH POSITIVE AFFIRMATIONS

The jury is still out on how many thoughts we have each day. There are credible studies that cite the number as being between 10,000 and 60,000! Even if the number is on the low end of the range, that's a lot of thoughts to process.

Negative thoughts get in the way of us doing what we want to or need to do. Have you noticed when you have a negative thought about something it's often followed by another negative thought, then another, and another, and soon you're not only in a bad mood, you've stopped doing anything productive. Before you know it, an hour has gone by and you've accomplished absolutely nothing.

Understanding the triggers of negative thought patterns and developing mechanisms for each one can help you avoid the slippery slope of negativity.

Trigger One: Thoughts as You're Waking Up

Your first thoughts when you wake up set the tone for the day.

Starting the day with the thought, "It's Monday, I can't believe how short the weekend was and now I have to go to work" sets you up to start your day on a negative note.

Starting the day with the thought, "What a great weekend. I got to spend time with my children and get some exercise."

Trigger Two: Thoughts as You're Looking in the Mirror While Getting Ready for Work

What you say to yourself when you look in the mirror affects your self-esteem. I promise you, there's no one who's completely satisfied with the image that stares back at them. If your best friend said to you what you say to yourself, I promise, you'd find another best friend.

Looking at the mirror and thinking, "You really need to lose weight" makes you feel bad about yourself and sets you up to be self-conscious about your weight for the rest of the day.

If you do need to lose weight look at the mirror and say out loud, "I'm in charge of everything I eat and drink and I make choices that reflect how I want to feel and my appearance," provides a boost of confidence that will help you stick to your goals.

Whenever you're standing in front of a mirror smile at yourself and say something positive about who you are or what you're going to accomplish that day.

Exercise V-4: Write a positive affirmation to say to yourself the next time you look in the mirror.

____

____

____

Trigger Three: Thoughts When Someone Berates You or Makes You Angry

It's tempting to blame someone else for your negative feelings; however, being angry is like drinking poison and hoping it will hurt the other person.

We have a choice in the way we process what's going on in the world around us. If you're looking for something to be unhappy about there will be no dearth of opportunity. A driver cuts you off in traffic, a clerk in a store is rude or inept, your client cancels a meeting at the last minute, etc. When these things happen, and they will, what you "say" to yourself and how you react will determine your mood. If it's negative, the "face" you're displaying to the rest of the world won't be a happy one.

I finally came to the realization that if someone else's actions upset me, I can:

- Find an effective way to address it with him/her (Effective=Positive),
- Change the way I internalize what he/she is doing (Effective=Positive),
- Let it go – he/she may be having a bad day (Effective=Positive),
- Stew about it, get angry, and make myself miserable (Ineffective=Negative).

Trigger Four: Thoughts When You Disappoint Yourself or Someone You Care About

Most of us, unbeknownst to the rest of the world, set fairly high standards for ourselves and take ourselves through the "would've, should've, could've" routine when we fail to live up to the person we want to be.

I'm no exception. My business required me to leave home to fly to a client site each Sunday afternoon and return home late Friday night. My weekends were a flurry of errands and chores and my to-do list kept growing.

I had very little time to see my family and friends during consulting engagements, and they often lasted for more than a year. At that point in time, I had several friends who, although I'd been travelling on this schedule since they'd known me, took it personally when I didn't see them every weekend.

One Saturday I joined a friend for dinner and a movie at her home. A few minutes into the movie I'd dozed off while sitting on her sofa. She woke me up when the movie ended and berated me for falling asleep. I'd apologized profusely but felt terrible.

The next morning, I felt the pang of guilt when I woke up. I was brushing my teeth when I looked in the mirror and saw an exhausted, stressed-out woman who was worn out from beating herself up for not being able to satisfy everyone else's needs.

I took a deep breath and told the woman looking back at me. "You're trying to do too many things instead of making the things you do count. If you had a client with this problem, you would know how to advise her. Now go sit down and figure it out." I immediately felt better and did just that.

When we're berating ourselves, whatever the reason, we're stuck in a useless cycle that can cause our confidence and mood to go into a negative spiral. It's important to remind ourselves that we have the wherewithal to understand how we've failed to live up to our own expectations and plan to either mend the situation or keep us from making the same mistake again.

Trigger Five: Thoughts When We're Stressed

Stress behaviors manifest themselves when we're afraid something bad is going to happen. Most of us have established stress behaviors that can run the gamut from completely shutting down to letting our tempers explode. Neither one is attractive, and both often have negative consequences.

Deciding to change a stress behavior that's not serving you well takes forethought and practice.

When you feel stressed about something, don't allow the situation to escalate before you take control of yourself. If you're with others and you can take a break without escalating the situation, take that opportunity.

If you're struggling for self-control and you're talking, end your next sentence as a question to give someone else the floor. Slow down your breathing and quietly take several deep breaths. If you can, sip some water.

Describe to yourself, as you would to someone else, what's going on in this situation and what it is you fear that's causing you to react this way. Try to recall being in a similar situation or watching someone else in similar situation when there was a successful resolution to the problem, and determine when it's appropriate to reengage.

If you're by yourself write out the problem that's causing you stress, your desired outcome, and what, if anything, you can do to bring about this outcome or mitigate the issue. Then write out a step-by-step plan of action.

Exercise V-5: Is there a Stress Behavior You Have That's Not Serving You Well? If So, Describe How You Plan to Use A Positive Approach to Resolve Stressful Issues.

____

____

____

____

____

STEP 3: STOP PROCRASTINATING

The Ted Talk

One thing I used to believe about myself was that I was a procrastinator and, indeed, people who are important to me reinforced that belief.

Then I watched a Ted Talk about procrastination by Tim Urban, a blogger whose '*Wait but Why'* blog explores procrastination. He described his early theory that procrastinators' brains were different than non-procrastinators'. You can check it out at: https://www.ted.com/talks/tim_urban_inside_the_mind_of_a_master_procrastinator

Urban tested this theory by arranging MRIs of his brain and a friend's who he believed was not a procrastinator. He described the results in a hilarious TED Talk; illustrated with pictures that looked to have been drawn by a fourth grader. Both brains had a Rational Decision Maker who is depicted with a steering wheel one would see on a ship; however, the procrastinator's brain also has an Instant Gratification Monkey. Every time a procrastinator starts to do something that's necessary to keep his ship on course, the Instant Gratification Monkey takes over, grabs the steering wheel and replaces it with an activity that's fun and completely non-productive, but quickly produces a visible result.

When a deadline approaches, the third character living in the procrastinator's brain, the Panic Monster, takes over and scares the Instant Gratification Monkey back up into his tree so the Rational Decision Maker can take over long enough for the activity to be completed, typically at an irrational pace.

Tim Urban goes on to explain that after the TED talk, he received thousands of emails from people (many with great accomplishments) saying they had the same problem and expressing frustration that they couldn't control their Monkey. Reading these made him realize there are two types of things we procrastinate about: those that have deadlines and those that don't, ***but we're all procrastinating about something!***

We all have a Rational Decision Maker, an Instant Gratification Monkey, and a Panic Monster in one form or another. The problem is that activities with no deadline don't wake up our Panic Monster. So, endeavors that involve some effort to get started but don't have a deadline - like taking care of your health, exercising, or tending to your relationships, can be left undone because they don't wake up the Panic Monster. These are the very activities that, when neglected, cause us no end of regrets, grief and unhappiness and can make us feel like spectators in our own lives.

The realization that everyone is procrastinating about something made me realize that I'm no different than anyone else. Procrastination is a manifestation of fear. It could be any fear: fear of failure, fear of embarrassment, even fear of going broke and being a bag lady. If you don't face it down and get on with it, you can cause the very thing you're afraid of to happen.

This understanding empowered me to determine that I could choose to quit letting myself be overwhelmed with everything I had to do and move on.

Exercise V-6: If, as Tim Urban says, "We're all procrastinating about something", what are you procrastinating about and what are you afraid of?

____

____

____

Exercise V-7: Complete this sentence: I would rather get on with (fill in with something you're procrastinating about) than (fill in something you're afraid of). For Example: I would rather (write the first chapter of my book) than (live with the regret of "what ifs").

I would rather _______________________ than ____________________________.

STEP 4: ADDRESS YOUR ADDICTIONS

If your dependence on alcohol, drugs, cigarettes, sex, social media, or Snickers is getting in the way of your financial success, your relationships, or what you want to do with your life, facing that dependency willbe a relief.

Even if there are no side effects yet but you know what you're doing will have long term implications, this might be the time to address the issue.

Addictions behave just like the Instant Gratification Monkey from Tim Urban's Ted Talk. Like any change, there's a process you can follow to make and positively approach that change.

Depending upon your addiction and the effect it's having on your life, you'll need to decide if you need help to quit, need to quit cold turkey, or just need to get it under control. If you decide to get help, do it. If you decide to quit cold turkey, do it. If you decide to control it, which is often where many of us start, then here's a process to determine if you have the where-with-all to do it on your own.

Imagine how different your life would be without the monkey being in the way of what you're trying to accomplish. I've found that once I acknowledge that my reason for change is more important to me than the addiction that's getting in the way of my happiness, I have a compelling reason to stick with beating the monkey. I know it's hard to gain traction with the weight of that monkey on my back.

Exercise V-8: Do you have an addiction that's getting in your way? If so are you willing to start the process of getting the proverbial "Monkey" off your back?

____

____

____

____

It's empowering to develop a positive affirmation to use to start each day. For example: "I am in charge of how much I drink. I can stay sober long enough to get what I need completed today." Say this positive affirmation every morning when you get up and call it into mind any time the Instant Gratification Monkey wants to take over.

Exercise V-9: Write a positive affirmation you can use to start each day.

____

____

____

____

If you're going to get the monkey under control, it's important to keep score so you know who's winning.

Exercise V-10: Establish Your Baseline. To establish your baseline, start by quantifying your average daily use and understanding the triggers that affect that usage. Use a journal and set up a section to record when you fed the monkey (drank, smoked, etc.), where you were, and why you fed your old habits.

Here's an Example:

At the end of the week (during your personal business meeting if you have one established) look at your journal and analyze your patterns. Count the total for each day and figure out the difference between what was going on during the days you fed the monkey the most and those you fed him the least. You might find that you feed him more on days when you are tired or on your days off. Next, analyze the trigger. The analysis might show you, "I often procrastinate when I have to make a phone call that will be frustrating" or "I always have drinks after work" or "I always have a cigarette before I take a shower". There's typically a recognizable trigger once you become aware of your pattern.

Now that you are beginning to understand use the lowest number as your goal. For the next two weeks make the commitment not to go over that number.

Exercise V-11: Begin to Cage the Monkey.

Best Day: ______ **Worst Day:** _________

Triggers:

____

____

____

____

____

Daily Goal for the Next Two Weeks: ___________________

Record your progress in your journal. If you let the monkey out of the cage for a day, take a minute and understand why. Don't make excuses, just review what happened, repeat your affirmation, and start again the next day.

Once you've successfully caged him, you can start to tame him by slowly limiting the amount and window of time he's allowed to play. Choose to either reduce the amount of your consumption or the times when you consume. For example, if you were smoking 30 cigarettes a day, reduce it by one to 29 a day; if you were having your first drink when you got up, wait an hour. (I found that if I got busy doing something on my list, an hour would fly by AND I'd gotten something done. Not a bad trade-off.)

Exercise V-12: Begin to Tame the Monkey. The Next Step I'm Going to Take to Tame This Monkey Is:

____

____

____

____

Over time, you'll figure out whether this is an addiction you can control or not. If you're making progress in the right direction, yet slipping up sometimes, just keep at it.

If you see no progress, it might be time to admit you can't do it on your own. There's no shame in that. Just find the type of help that will work for you. It takes more strength to confront an issue than it does to fight it.

STEP 5: TREAT YOURSELF BETTER

The next category of behaviors where we get in our own way are the ones associated with the choices we make or fail to make.

Get Good Sleep: If you're not one of the minority who go to work at the same time every day, five days a week, getting enough sleep requires attention.

I don't know about you, but when I haven't had enough sleep nothing is any fun, everything irritates me, and I feel like I'm phoning it in. I found that just a few changes in my personal habits help ensure when I have time to sleep that I actively relax enough to do so.

- **Step 1: Establish A Quiet Time.** Be certain to let your friends and family know when your quiet time is. Trust me when I tell you, they'll be thrilled to know you're not going to be answering their calls after 8:30 PM because you're sleeping. I was startled when I finally started to tell my friends that I have trouble staying up past 8:30 and took the time to understand when they liked to talk. They enjoyed a bit of humor at my expense and I was relieved they were no longer irritated when I called them back during the time that suited them best the next day.

  Once you establish a quiet time, even if you can't sleep, use the time for yourself. Read a book, watch a movie, play with your cat, but unplug. You're worth 20 minutes spent on yourself, right?

- **Step 2: Establish a Sleep Routine.** Our minds are wired to recognize patterns of behavior. They recognize "put on my sleep clothes, take out my contacts, wash my face, brush my teeth" as what we do when we get ready to sleep.

- **Step 3: Establish a Pleasant Sleep Place.** The place you sleep should be personalized for what helps you relax (have you ever noticed that sometimes when you have an overnight guest or sleep somewhere else you're still tired when you get up?). If clutter irritates you, declutter. Give yourself the gift of clean sheets and a clean pillow. The quality of your sleep will determine how tomorrow goes and how you approach it.

Exercise V-13: What is one thing you can change or do differently that will improve your sleep?

____

____

Eat and Drink Wisely. Just face it…most Americans should eat better. Much of what we eat is fast food that's breaded, deep fried, covered in cheese, has loads of sodium, calories, and very few nutrients. In other words, we eat like we're five years old.

Other than the fact that if this is the way we're eating we're probably exhausted all the time because we're not getting the nutrients our body needs and are setting ourselves up for a miserable old age of medical complaints, why would we attempt to do better?

Changing that behavior isn't going to happen overnight, but wouldn't it be great to start feeding your body what it needs to be happy? You can start to change and very quickly you'll start to see quantifiable benefits.

- **Step 1: Learn to Cook One Healthy Meal.** In case no one ever mentioned it, being able to cook a healthy and delicious meal is worth the effort. Even if it's only a pre-cooked chicken, salad, and a side, you'll feel better after you've made it and reap the benefits after you've eaten it.

Add one healthy meal to your repertoire every month. It doesn't have to be complicated.

- **Step 2: Learn to Eat Green Food.** When my son was five his kindergarten class listened to a presentation on food safety. At dinner that night he looked solemnly at the spinach on his plate and announced, "I don't eat green food." He stuck to that for years and wouldn't even eat green Jell-O.

  Fresh vegetables are one of the nicest things we can do to make our bodies healthy. You might start with only one a week but figuring out how to get one into a meal every day is worth it.

  One of the benefits of most green foods is they help keep us "regular" and that alone is worth incorporating them into our diet.

Exercise V-14: What one thing can you change, or do differently that will improve what you eat and drink?

____

____

- **Check In With Your Doc.** Partner with your primary care doctor so he or she can help you stay well instead of treating you only when you're sick. We're all a little bit different and when there's a change in your lab values, it may not be noticed if you don't go in for a check-up once a year while you're well and establish your norms.

  By building a regular relationship with your primary care doctor, when you're sick he/she can tell what's changed in your body chemistry that might be causing any problem you might have. The doctor might find a change in your body chemistry early on that otherwise wouldn't have been noticed.

  If you only ever see a doctor at an acute care clinic or, worse yet, emergency room, they're treating the illness rather than working to keep you well. They're helping treat the symptoms instead of helping you identify and combat the cause.

- **Save Your Smile.** Did you know that one of the methods of assessing the health of an animal is their dental health? Human animals are no different. In fact, the US Armed Forces won't deploy a service member to a combat zone until any dental issues are corrected.

Yet many of us don't visit the dentist regularly. A little cavity caught at six months can easily be fixed. By the time it starts to bother you it's often already touching a nerve and requires invasive care that can weaken the structure of the tooth.

A professional dental cleaning every six months keeps plaque and bacteria from homesteading in your mouth. This helps to prevent not only cavities but also gum disease.

The kicker here is preventive dental care is typically covered by dental insurance policies that cost about $30 a month, whereas remedial dental care is never fully covered and can cost the price of a new car.

Another preventive measure is to leave the sugary caffeine drinks that permeate your dental enamel in the convenience store. They are an insidious threat to your dental health and they're ridiculously expensive. Caffeine, guanine and taurine aren't worth $4.95 for 8 ounces and an hour of feeling decent before you crash and fall.

Who in their right mind thinks having their teeth sit in a cleaning mixture by their sink every night is sexy?

STEP 6: MANAGE YOUR STRESS

It's obvious that life today is more stressful than ever before. I attribute this to the constant barrage of information coming our way. We have so much stimuli shoved in our faces all the time that it's acutely uncomfortable when we try to disconnect and give ourselves a little attention or time to relax, settle, and reset.

It's essential to develop the willingness and ability to quiet your mind. Years ago, a mentor recommended The Four Agreements, by Don Miguel Ruiz. The book offers readers four agreements you can make with yourself that, if followed, have a profound effect upon how you live your life and the effect other people have on you.

"Be Impeccable With Your Word", the first of these agreements, is so basic and rudimentary one would expect it to be a baseline tenet of our lives. As with any lesson, the approach you take to applying it to your life is based upon what it means to you. Being impeccable with your word takes many forms and has many implications.

- **Tell the truth.** We each know when we're telling the truth and when we're stretching it. Whether I'm representing myself or the business I'm working for, there should be only one version of the truth as I see it. It involves acknowledging what I understand to be true might not be someone else's truth and that it's wise to be open to understanding their perspective.

- **Keep commitments.** This is something that's essential to improving the probability you'll be successful and it's easy to start addressing. Only make commitments you believe you can meet. Once you've made a commitment, do everything within your power to meet it, whether it's to a client, colleague, friend, or family member. If you find for some reason you can't meet your commitment, be honest with the person and tell them why and when they can expect the promised results.

- **Do a fair day's work.** When you are working, put in the required and expected effort. Don't waste time.

- **Produce the service your customers expect.** Don't take short cuts on the quality of your service. It represents who you are.

  No one wants to work with someone they can't trust. Be impeccable with your word and people will come to trust you because they know they can depend upon you to be honest regardless of the cost.

"Do Your Best Everyday" is the second agreement. Making and following this agreement is the best method I know to rid yourself of the guilt that comes with any type of failure. We can all recall circumstances in our lives when we didn't do our best. Either we were tired, overwhelmed, or just didn't have the energy to make the effort to show up and do our best.

Like anything else, doing your best requires practice. You can focus on these simple steps:

- **Manage your time.** Mindlessly surfing the web, gossiping with a co-worker, complaining about "them", whoever "they" may be, checking social media, or texting your friends all take time away from the time available to make a difference. Go in with a plan for what you're going to accomplish each day and do those things first.

- **Do one thing at a time.** Multi-tasking assures that everything you do takes longer. Even with large, multi-day or week-long efforts, decide a logical cut-off point between completing one activity and starting another, then work to that point before moving on to something else.

- **Do quality work.** This doesn't mean perfection, but it does mean producing a product that meets the requirements for which it was intended. You should be proud of anything you produce; making sure it's a quality product takes as much effort as phoning it in.

  Doing your best everyday means just that – with what I know and what I have to offer, this is the best I can do. I can take pride in the effort I gave, whether the result was a success or not.

"If You Have a Question, Ask", the third agreement, prevents misperceptions from becoming disagreements. When I read this the first time I recalled situations where I'd sensed someone had slighted or wronged me in some way and blew it out of proportion instead of simply asking the person if he meant for me to perceive it that way.

Typically, the person either meant no harm or hadn't considered the implications from someone else's perspective. For example, a company you've done work for is more than 30 days behind on their payments. When you place a call to their accounting office you're told the client who needs to approve your invoice has yet to do so. If your client values your contribution, he probably has overlooked the invoice so it's important you contact him about it. If he did intend it, you would want to know that, so you could either attempt to make it right or understand why you've lost a client.

"Nothing Anyone Else Does Is About You", the fourth agreement, was the agreement that had the most profound effect on my professional relationships. If nothing anyone else does is about me, what in the world was I thinking when I tried to guilt other people into action or make excuses for my own issues by walking around with a 'V' on my forehead. (The 'V', of course, stands for VICTIM.)

Before I understood this agreement, I'd spent a lot of time thinking:

- "If only she would do this, or he would stop doing that, my business would be a success."

- "If only this would happen or that hadn't happened, I would have won that bid."

Then there was the ominous "they":

- "They" stood in the way of my success.
- "They" could afford to undercut my bid or put more people on any job.

After internalizing this, I realized I was wasting energy I needed to be successful by worrying about the effect other people were having on me rather than focusing on what I needed to do to make my business successful.

By following these four agreements, I finally started to get out of my own way.

Exercise V-15: List three things you can do to incorporate The Four Agreements into your current situation to be more successful and reduce your stress level.

1. ____

____

2. ____

____

3. ____

____

ACKNOWLEDGEMENTS

Anthony Lee, you're my inspiration for how opening a low-cost business start-up can be a life changing experience. I'm proud of you for taking the steps to do it.

Tina Atkinson, thank you for giving me the freedom to work on this by taking care of the home front so I was free to spend time on the island and get this done, and for the gift of your precious time to edit the manuscript.

Fran Willis White, your coaching during our daily sessions kept me going and gave me the energy to complete this project. You clarify and strengthen my message.

My friends at UUCJ Fernandina Beach for encouraging my dream of producing this workbook as a tool to facilitate income equality.

My brother, D. Razor Babb, the real writer in the family, who inspired me to share his vision for criminal justice reform

The staff and members of the Fernandina Beach – Nassau Chamber of Commerce for their encouragement, friendship, and support of the small business community.

ABOUT THE AUTHOR

Leah Ward-Lee

Author's Photo by: Gerry Burns, www.GerryBurns.com

Leah Ward-Lee is a serial micro-entrepreneur. She opened her first business at ten after lobbying for and receiving a shoe shine kit for Christmas. She pulled her wagon through the neighborhood, going door-to-door, offering to shine her neighbor's shoes for twenty-five cents a pair. Once her wagon was full, she took the shoes home and polished them.

Unfortunately, that business was short-lived. She hadn't tagged the shoes and couldn't remember whose shoes were whose, so her dad went with her to retrace the route until every pair was returned.

Since then she's had businesses developing and teaching college courses, instructing aerobic classes, owning half a plane that was rented to a flight and maintenance school, and renting homes. She's also owned a consignment store, a gift shop, a gift basket business, a consulting firm, hosted *The Executive Toolbox* (a weekly radio show), and a publishing company.

She served twenty years in the US Army, served as the Chief Information and Technical Officer for two major financial services corporations, and had a second career as a management consultant.

Leah resides on Amelia Island with Sammy and Goliath, her two rescue dogs.

Follow Leah at *www.1000dollarstartups.com*

www.ingramcontent.com/pod-product-compliance
Lightning Source LLC
Chambersburg PA
CBHW051216200326
41519CB00025B/7139

* 9 7 8 1 9 4 5 4 8 4 0 7 0 *